Prickly Paradigm Press, LLC is the North American successor of Prickly Pear Press, founded in Britain by Keith Hart and Anna Grimshaw in 1993. Prickly Paradigm aims to follow their lead in publishing challenging and sometimes outrageous pamphlets, not only on anthropology, but on other academic disciplines, the arts, and the contemporary world.

Prickly Paradigm is marketed and distributed by The University of Chicago Press.

www.press.uchicago.edu

A list of current and future titles, as well as contact addresses for all correspondence, can be found on our website and at the back of this pamphlet.

www.prickly-paradigm.com

Executive Publisher
Marshall Sahlins

Publishers
Peter Sahlins
Ramona Naddaff
Bernard Sahlins
Seminary Co-op Bookstore

Editor
Matthew Engelke
info@prickly-paradigm.com

Design and layout by Bellwether Manufacturing.

T0019638

Fragments of an
Anarchist Anthropology

Fragments of an Anarchist Anthropology

David Graeber

PRICKLY PARADIGM PRESS
CHICAGO

Prickly Paradigm Press, LLC
5629 South University Avenue
Chicago, Il 60637

www.prickly-paradigm.com

ISBN: 0-9728196-4-9
LCCN: 2004090746

Printed in the United States of America on acid-free
paper.

Anarchism:

The name given to a principle or theory of life and conduct under which society is conceived without government—harmony in such a society being obtained, not by submission to law, or by obedience to any authority, but by free agreements concluded between the various groups, territorial and professional, freely constituted for the sake of production and consumption, as also for the satisfaction of the infinite variety of needs and aspirations of a civilized being.

Peter Kropotkin (*Encyclopedia Brittanica*)

Basically, if you're not a utopianist, you're a schmuck.

Jonothon Feldman (*Indigenous Planning Times*)

What follows are a series of thoughts, sketches of potential theories, and tiny manifestos—all meant to offer a glimpse at the outline of a body of radical theory that does not actually exist, though it might possibly exist at some point in the future.

Since there are very good reasons why an anarchist anthropology really ought to exist, we might start by asking why one doesn't—or, for that matter, why an anarchist sociology doesn't exist, or an anarchist economics, anarchist literary theory, or anarchist political science.

Why are there so few anarchists in the academy?

It's a pertinent question because, as a political philosophy, anarchism is veritably exploding right now. Anarchist or anarchist-inspired movements are growing everywhere; traditional anarchist principles—autonomy, voluntary association, self-organization, mutual aid, direct democracy—have gone from the basis for organizing within the globalization movement, to playing the same role in radical movements of all kinds everywhere. Revolutionaries in Mexico, Argentina, India, and elsewhere have increasingly abandoned even talking about seizing power, and begun to formulate radically different ideas of what a revolution would even mean. Most, admittedly, fall shy of actually using the word "anarchist." But as Barbara Epstein has recently pointed out anarchism has by now largely taken the place Marxism had in the social movements of the '60s: even those who do not consider themselves anarchists feel they have to define themselves in relation to it, and draw on its ideas.

Yet all this has found almost no reflection in the academy. Most academics seem to have only the vaguest idea what anarchism is even about; or dismiss it with the crudest stereotypes. ("Anarchist organization! But isn't that a contradiction in terms?") In the United States there are thousands of academic Marxists of one sort or another, but hardly a dozen scholars willing openly to call themselves anarchists.

So are academics just behind the curve here? It's possible. Perhaps in a few years the academy will be overrun by anarchists. But I'm not holding my breath. It does seem that Marxism has an affinity with the academy that anarchism never will. It was, after all, the only great social movement that was invented by a Ph.D., even if afterwards, it became a movement intending to rally the working class. Most accounts of the history of anarchism assume it was basically similar: anarchism is presented as the brainchild of certain nineteenth-century thinkers—Proudhon, Bakunin, Kropotkin, etc.—it then went on to inspire working-class organizations, became enmeshed in political struggles, divided into sects... Anarchism, in the standard accounts, usually comes out as Marxism's poorer cousin, theoretically a bit flat-footed but making up for brains, perhaps, with passion and sincerity. But in fact, the analogy is strained at best. The nineteenth-century "founding figures" did not think of themselves as having invented anything particularly new. The basic principles of anarchism—self-organization, voluntary association, mutual aid—referred to forms of human behavior they assumed to have been around about as long as humanity. The same goes for the rejection of the state and of all forms of structural violence, inequality, or domination (anarchism literally means "without rulers"), even the assumption that all these forms are somehow related and reinforce each other. None of it was presented as some startling new doctrine. And in fact it was not: one can find records of people making similar arguments throughout history, despite the fact there is every reason to believe that in most times and places, such opinions were the ones least likely to be written down. We are talking less about a body of theory, then, than about an attitude, or perhaps one might even say a faith: the rejection of certain types of social relations, the confidence that certain others would be much better ones on which to build a livable society, the belief that such a society could actually exist.

Even if one compares the historical schools of Marxism, and anarchism, one can see we are dealing with a fundamentally different sort of project. Marxist schools have authors. Just as Marxism sprang from the mind of Marx, so we have Leninists, Maoists, Trotksyites, Gramscians, Althusserians... (Note how the list starts with heads of state and grades almost seamlessly into French professors.) Pierre Bourdieu once noted that, if the academic field is a game in which scholars strive for dominance, then you know you have won when other scholars start wondering how to make an adjective out of your name. It is, presumably, to preserve the possibility of winning the game that intellectuals insist, in discussing each other, on continuing to employ just the sort of Great Man theories of history they would scoff at in just about any other context: Foucault's ideas, like Trotsky's, are never treated as primarily the products of a certain intellectual milieu, as something that emerged from endless conversations and arguments involving hundreds of people, but always, as if they emerged from the genius of a single man (or, very occasionally, woman). It's not quite either that Marxist politics organized itself like an academic discipline or that it has become a model for how radical intellectuals, or increasingly, all intellectuals, treated one another; rather, the two developed somewhat in tandem. From the perspective of the academy, this led to many salutary results—the feeling there should be some moral center, that academic concerns should be relevant to people's lives—but also, many disastrous ones: turning much intellectual debate into a kind of parody of sectarian politics, with everyone trying to reduce each others' arguments into ridiculous caricatures so as to declare them not only wrong, but also evil and dangerous—even if the debate is usually taking place in language so arcane that no one who could not afford seven years of grad school would have any way of knowing the debate was going on.

Now consider the different schools of anarchism. There are Anarcho-Syndicalists, Anarcho-Communists, Insurrectionists, Cooperativists, Individualists, Platformists... None are named after some Great Thinker; instead, they are invariably named either after some kind of practice, or most often, organizational principle. (Significantly, those Marxist tendencies which are not named after individuals, like Autonomism or Council Communism, are also the ones closest to anarchism.) Anarchists like to distinguish themselves by what they do, and how they organize themselves to go about doing it. And indeed this has always been what anarchists have spent most of their time thinking and arguing about. Anarchists have never been much interested in the kinds of broad strategic or philosophical questions that have historically preoccupied Marxists—questions like: Are the peasants a potentially revolutionary class? (Anarchists consider this something for the peasants to decide.) What is the nature of the commodity form? Rather, they tend to argue with each other about what is the truly democratic way to go about a meeting, at what point organization stops being empowering and starts squelching individual freedom. Or, alternately, about the ethics of opposing power: What is direct action? Is it necessary (or right) to publicly condemn someone who assassinates a head of state? Or can assassination, especially if it prevents something terrible, like a war, be a moral act? When is it okay to break a window?

To sum up then:

1. Marxism has tended to be a theoretical or analytical discourse about revolutionary strategy.
2. Anarchism has tended to be an ethical discourse about revolutionary practice.

Obviously, everything I've said has been something of a caricature (there have been wildly sectarian anarchist groups, and plenty of libertarian, practice-oriented Marxists including, arguably, myself). Still, even so stated, this does suggest a great deal of potential complementarity between the two. And indeed there has been: even Mikhail Bakunin, for all his endless battles with Marx over practical questions, also personally translated Marx's *Capital* into Russian. But it also makes it easier to understand why there are so few anarchists in the academy. It's not just that anarchism does not tend to have much use for high theory. It's that it is primarily concerned with forms of practice; it insists, before anything else, that one's means must be consonant with one's ends; one cannot create freedom through authoritarian means; in fact, as much as possible, one must oneself, in one's relations with one's friends and allies, embody the society one wishes to create. This does not square very well with operating within the university, perhaps the only Western institution other than the Catholic Church and British monarchy that has survived in much the same form from the Middle Ages, doing intellectual battle at conferences in expensive hotels, and trying to pretend all this somehow furthers revolution. At the very least, one would imagine being an openly anarchist professor would mean challenging the way universities are run—and I don't mean by demanding an anarchist studies department, either—and that, of course, is going to get one in far more trouble than anything one could ever write.

This does not mean anarchist theory is impossible.

This doesn't mean anarchists have to be *against* theory. After all, anarchism is, itself, an idea, even if a very old one. It is also a project, which sets out to begin creating the institutions of a new society "within the shell of the old," to expose, subvert, and undermine structures of domination but always, while doing so, proceeding in a democratic fashion, a manner which itself demonstrates those structures are unnecessary. Clearly any such project has need of the tools of intellectual analysis and understanding. It might not need

High Theory, in the sense familiar today. Certainly it will not need one single, Anarchist High Theory. That would be completely inimical to its spirit. Much better, I think, something more in the spirit of anarchist decision-making processes, employed in anything from tiny affinity groups to gigantic spokescouncils of thousands of people. Most anarchist groups operate by a consensus process which has been developed, in many ways, to be the exact opposite of the high-handed, divisive, sectarian style so popular amongst other radical groups. Applied to theory, this would mean accepting the need for a diversity of high theoretical perspectives, united only by certain shared commitments and understandings. In consensus process, everyone agrees from the start on certain broad principles of unity and purposes for being for the group; but beyond that they also accept as a matter of course that no one is ever going to convert another person completely to their point of view, and probably shouldn't try; and that therefore discussion should focus on concrete questions of action, and coming up with a plan that everyone can live with and no one feels is in fundamental violation of their principles. One could see a parallel here: a series of diverse perspectives, joined together by their shared desire to understand the human condition, and move it in the direction of greater freedom. Rather than be based on the need to prove others' fundamental assumptions wrong, it seeks to find particular projects on which they reinforce each other. Just because theories are incommensurable in certain respects does not mean they cannot exist or even reinforce each other, any more than the fact that individuals have unique and incommensurable views of the world means they cannot become friends, or lovers, or work on common projects.

Even more than High Theory, what anarchism needs is what might be called Low Theory: a way of grappling with those real, immediate questions that emerge from a transformative project. Mainstream social science actually isn't much help here, because normally in mainstream social science this sort of thing is generally classified as "policy issues," and no self-respecting anarchist would have anything to do with these.

against policy (a tiny manifesto):
The notion of "policy" presumes a state or governing apparatus which imposes its will on others. "Policy" is the negation of politics; policy is by definition something concocted by some form of elite, which presumes it knows better than others how their affairs are to be conducted. By participating in policy debates the very best one can achieve is to limit the damage, since the very premise is inimical to the idea of people managing their own affairs.

So in this case, the question becomes: What sort of social theory would actually be of interest to those who are trying to help bring about a world in which people are free to govern their own affairs?

This is what this pamphlet is mainly about.

For starters, I would say any such theory would have to begin with some initial assumptions. Not many. Probably just two. First, it would have to proceed from the assumption that, as the Brazilian folk song puts it, "another world is possible." That institutions like the state, capitalism, racism and male dominance are not inevitable; that it would be possible to have a world in which these things would not exist, and that we'd all be better off as a result. To commit oneself to such a principle is almost an act of faith, since how can one have certain knowledge of such matters? It might possibly turn out that such a world is *not* possible. But one could also make the argument that it's this very unavailability of absolute knowledge which makes a commitment to optimism a moral imperative: Since one cannot know a radically better world is not possible, are we not betraying everyone by insisting on continuing to justify, and reproduce, the mess we have today? And anyway, even if we're wrong, we might well get a lot closer.

> **against anti-utopianism (another tiny manifesto):**
> Here of course one has to deal with the inevitable objection: that utopianism has lead to unmitigated horror, as Stalinists, Maoists, and other idealists tried to carve society into impossible shapes, killing millions in the process.

This argument belies a fundamental misconception: that imagining better worlds was itself the problem. Stalinists and their ilk did not kill because they dreamed great dreams—actually, Stalinists were famous for being rather short on imagination—but because they mistook their dreams for scientific certainties. This led them to feel they had a right to impose their visions through a machinery of violence. Anarchists are proposing nothing of the sort, on either count. They presume no inevitable course of history and one can never further the course of freedom by creating new forms of coercion. In fact all forms of systemic violence are (among other things) assaults on the role of the imagination as a political principle, and the only way to begin to think about eliminating systematic violence is by recognizing this.

And of course one could write very long books about the atrocities throughout history carried out by cynics and other pessimists...

So that's the first proposition. The second, I'd say, is that any anarchist social theory would have to reject self-consciously any trace of vanguardism. The role of intellectuals is most definitely not to form an elite that can arrive at the correct strategic analyses and then lead the masses to follow. But if not that, what? This is one reason I'm calling this essay "Fragments of an Anarchist *Anthropology*"—because this is one area where I think anthropology is particularly well positioned to help. And not only because most actually-existing self-governing communities, and actually-existing non-market economies in the world have been investigated by anthropologists rather than sociologists or historians. It is also because the practice of ethnography provides at least something of a model, if a very rough, incipient model, of how non-vanguardist revolutionary intellectual practice might work. When one carries out an ethnography, one observes what people do, and then tries to tease out the hidden symbolic, moral, or pragmatic logics that underlie their actions; one tries to get at the way people's habits and actions makes sense in ways that they are not themselves completely aware of. One obvious role for a radical intellectual is to do precisely that: to look at those who are creating viable alternatives, try to figure out what might be the larger implications of what they are (already) doing, and then offer those ideas back, not as prescriptions, but as contributions, possibilities—as gifts. This is more or less what I was trying to do a few paragraphs ago when I suggested that social theory could refashion itself in the manner of direct democratic process. And as that example makes clear, such a project would actually have to have two aspects, or moments if you like: one ethnographic, one utopian, suspended in a constant dialogue.

None of this has much to do with what anthropology, even radical anthropology, has actually been like over the last hundred years or so. Still, there has been a strange affinity, over the years, between anthropology and anarchism which is in itself significant.

Graves, Brown, Mauss, Sorel

It's not so much that anthropologists embraced anarchism, or even, were consciously espousing anarchist ideas; it's more that they moved in the same circles, their ideas tended to bounce off one another, that there was something about anthropological thought in particular—its keen awareness of the very range of human possibilities—that gave it an affinity to anarchism from the very beginning.

Let me start with Sir James Frazer, even though he was the furthest thing from an anarchist. Frazer, chair of anthropology in Cambridge at the turn of the (last) century, was a classic stodgy Victorian who wrote accounts of savage customs, based mainly on the results of questionnaires sent out to missionaries and colonial officials. His ostensible theoretical attitude was utterly condescending—he believed almost all magic, myth and ritual was based on foolish logical mistakes—but his magnum opus, *The Golden Bough*, contained such florid, fanciful, and strangely beautiful descriptions of tree spirits, eunuch priests, dying vegetation gods, and the sacrifice of divine kings, that he inspired a generation of poets and literati. Among them was Robert Graves, a British poet who first became famous for writing bitingly satirical verse from the trenches of World War I. At the end of the war, Graves ended up in a hospital in France where he was cured of shell shock by W. H. R. Rivers, the British anthropologist famous for the Torres Straits Expedition, who doubled as a psychiatrist. Graves was so impressed by Rivers that he was later to suggest professional anthropologists be placed in charge of all world governments. Not a particularly anarchist sentiment, certainly—but Graves tended to dart about between all sorts of odd political positions. In the end, he was to abandon "civilization"—industrial society—entirely and spend the last fifty years or so of his life in a village on the Spanish island of Majorca, supporting himself by writing novels, but also producing numerous books of love poetry, and a series of some of the most subversive essays ever written.

Graves' thesis was, among other things, that greatness was a pathology; "great men" were essentially destroyers and "great" poets not much better (his arch-enemies were Virgil, Milton and Pound), that all real poetry is and has always been a mythic celebration of an ancient Supreme Goddess, of whom Frazer had only confused glimmerings, and whose matriarchal followers were conquered and destroyed by Hitler's beloved Aryan hoards when they emerged from the Ukrainian Steppes in the early Bronze Age (though they survived a bit longer in Minoan Crete). In a book called *The White Goddess: An Historical Grammar of Poetic Myth*, he claimed to map out the rudiments of her calendar rites in different parts of Europe, focusing on the periodic ritual murder of the Goddess' royal consorts, among other things a surefire way of guaranteeing would-be great men do not get out of hand, and ending the book with a call for an eventual industrial collapse. I say "claimed" advisedly here. The delightful, if also confusing, thing about

Graves' books is that he's obviously having so much fun writing them, throwing out one outrageous thesis after another, that it's impossible to tell how much of it is meant to be taken seriously. Or whether that's even a meaningful question. In one essay, written in the '50s, Graves invents the distinction between "reasonableness" and "rationality" later made famous by Stephen Toulmin in the '80s, but he does it in the course of an essay written to defend Socrates' wife, Xanthippe, from her reputation as an atrocious nag. (His argument: imagine you had been married to Socrates.)

Did Graves really believe that women are always superior to men? Did he really expect us to believe he had solved one mythical problem by falling into an "analeptic trance" and overhearing a conversation about fish between a Greek historian and Roman official in Cyprus in 54 CE? It's worth wondering, because for all their current obscurity, in these writings, Graves essentially invented two different intellectual traditions which were later to become major theoretical strains in modern anarchism—if admittedly, generally considered two of the most *outré*. On the one hand, the cult of the Great Goddess has been revived and become a direct inspiration for Pagan Anarchism, hippyish performers of spiral dances who are always welcome at mass actions because they do seem to have rather a knack for influencing the weather; on the other, Primitivists, whose most famous (and extreme) avatar is John Zerzan, who has taken Graves' rejection of industrial civilization and hopes for general economic collapse even further, arguing that even agriculture was a great historical mistake. Both the Pagans and the Primitivists, curiously, share exactly that ineffable quality which makes Graves' work so distinctive: it's really impossible to know on what level one is supposed to read it. It's both ridiculous self-parody, and terribly serious, at the same time.

There have also been anthropologists—among them, some of the founding figures of the discipline—who have themselves dabbled with anarchist, or anarchistic, politics.

The most notorious case was that of a turn of the century student named Al Brown, known to his college friends as "Anarchy Brown." Brown was an admirer of the famous anarchist Prince (he of course renounced his title), Peter Kropotkin, arctic explorer and naturalist, who had thrown social Darwinism into a tumult from which it still has never quite recovered by documenting how the most successful species tend to be those which cooperate the most effectively. (Sociobiology for instance was basically an attempt to come up with an answer to Kropotkin.) Later, Brown was to begin affecting a cloak and a monocle, adopting a fancy mock-aristocratic hyphenated name (A. R. Radcliffe-Brown), and ultimately, in the 1920s and '30s, becoming the master theorist of British social anthropology. The older Brown didn't like to talk too much about his youthful politics, but it's probably no coincidence that his main theoretical interest remained the maintenance of social order outside the state.

Perhaps the most intriguing case though is that of Marcel Mauss, Radcliffe-Brown's contemporary, and the inventor of French anthropology. Mauss was a child of Orthodox Jewish parents who had the mixed blessing of also being the nephew of Emile Durkheim, the founder of French sociology. Mauss was also a revolutionary socialist. For much of his life, he managed a consumer coop in Paris, and was constantly writing screeds for socialist newspapers, carrying out projects of research on coops in other countries, and trying to create links between coops in order to build an alternative, anti-capitalist, economy. His most famous work was written in response to the crisis of socialism he saw in Lenin's reintroduction of the market in the Soviet Union in the '20s: If it was impossible to simply legislate the money economy away, even in Russia, the least monetarized society in Europe, then perhaps revolutionaries needed to start looking at the ethnographic record to see what sort of creature the market really was, and what viable alternatives to capitalism might look like. Hence his "Essay on the Gift," written in 1925, which argued (among other things) that the origin of all contracts lies in communism, an unconditional commitment to another's needs, and that despite endless economic textbooks to the contrary, there has never been an economy based on barter: that actually-existing societies which do not employ money have instead been gift economies in which the distinctions we now make between interest and altruism, person and property, freedom and obligation, simply did not exist.

Mauss believed socialism could never be built by state fiat but only gradually, from below, that it was possible to begin building a new society based on mutual aid and self-organization "in the shell of the old"; he felt that existing popular practices provided the basis both for a moral critique of capitalism and possible glimpses of what that future society would be like. All of these are classic anarchist positions. Still, he did not consider himself an anarchist. In fact, he never had anything good to say about them. This was, it appears, because he identified anarchism mainly with the figure of Georges Sorel, an apparently quite personally distasteful French anarcho-syndicalist and anti-Semite, now mainly famous for his essay *Reflections sur le Violence*. Sorel argued that since the masses were not fundamentally good or rational, it was foolish to make one's primary appeal to them through reasoned arguments. Politics is the art of inspiring others with great myths. For revolutionaries, he proposed the myth of an apocalyptic General Strike, a moment of total transformation. To maintain it, he added, one would need a revolutionary elite capable of keeping the myth alive by their willingness to engage in symbolic acts of violence—an elite which, like the Marxist vanguard party (often somewhat less symbolic in its violence), Mauss described as a kind of perpetual conspiracy, a modern version of the secret political men's societies of the ancient world.

In other words, Mauss saw Sorel, and hence anarchism, as introducing an element of the irrational, of violence, and of vanguardism. It might seem a bit odd that among French revolutionaries of the time, it should have been the trade unionist emphasizing the power of myth, and the anthropologist objecting, but in the context of the '20s and '30s, with fascist stirrings everywhere, it's understandable why a European radical—especially a Jewish one—might see all this as just a little creepy. Creepy enough to throw cold water even on the otherwise rather appealing image of the General Strike—which is after all about the least violent possible way to imagine an apocalyptic revolution. By the '40s, Mauss concluded his suspicions had proved altogether justified.

To the doctrine of the revolutionary vanguard, he wrote, Sorel added a notion originally culled from Mauss' own uncle Durkheim: a doctrine of corporatism, of vertical structures glued together by techniques of social solidarity. This he said was a great influence on Lenin, by Lenin's own admission. From there it was adopted by the Right. By the end of his life, Sorel himself had become increasingly sympathetic with fascism; in this he followed the same trajectory as Mussolini (another youthful dabbler with anarcho-syndicalism) and who, Mauss believed, took these same Durkheimian/Sorelian/Leninist ideas to their ultimate conclusions. By the end of his life, Mauss became convinced even Hitler's great ritual pageants, torch-lit parades with their chants of "*Seig Heil!*," were really inspired by accounts he and his uncle had written about totemic rituals of Australian aborigines. "When we were describing how ritual can create social solidarity, of submerging the individual in the mass," he complained, "it never occurred to us that anyone would apply such techniques in the modern day!" (In fact, Mauss was mistaken. Modern research has shown Nuremberg rallies were actually inspired by Harvard pep rallies. But this is another story.) The outbreak of war destroyed Mauss, who had never completely recovered from losing most of his closest friends in the First World War. When the Nazis took Paris he refused to flee, but sat in his office every day with a pistol in his desk, waiting for the Gestapo to arrive. They never did, but the terror, and weight of his feelings of historical complicity, finally shattered his sanity.

The anarchist anthropology that almost already does exist

In the end, though, Marcel Mauss has probably had more influence on anarchists than all the other ones combined. This is because he was interested in alternative moralities, which opened the way to thinking that societies without states and markets were the way they were because they actively wished to live that way. Which in our terms means, because they were anarchists. Insofar as fragments of an anarchist anthropology do, already, exist, they largely derive from him.

Before Mauss, the universal assumption had been that economies without money or markets had operated by means of "barter"; they were trying to engage in market behavior (acquire useful goods and services at the least cost to themselves, get rich if possible...), they just hadn't yet developed very sophisticated ways of going about it. Mauss demonstrated that in fact, such economies were really "gift economies." They were not based on calculation, but on a refusal to calculate; they were rooted in an ethical system which consciously rejected most of what we would consider the basic principles of economics. It was not that they had not yet learned to seek profit through the most efficient means. They would have found the very premise that the point of an economic transaction—at least, one with someone who was not your enemy—was to seek the greatest profit deeply offensive.

It is significant that the one (of the few) overtly anarchist anthropologists of recent memory, another Frenchman, Pierre Clastres, became famous for making a similar argument on the political level. He insisted political anthropologists had still not completely gotten over the old evolutionist perspectives that saw the state primarily as a more sophisticated form of organization than what had come before; stateless peoples, such as the Amazonian societies Clastres studied, were tacitly assumed not to have attained the level of say, the Aztecs or the Inca. But what if, he proposed, Amazonians were not entirely unaware of what the elementary forms of state power might be like—what it would mean to allow some men to give everyone else orders which could not be questioned, since they were backed up by the threat of force—and were for that very reason determined to ensure such things never came about? What if they considered the fundamental premises of our political science morally objectionable?

The parallels between the two arguments are actually quite striking. In gift economies there are, often, venues for enterprising individuals: But everything is arranged in such a way they could never be used as a platform for creating permanent inequalities of wealth, since self-aggrandizing types all end up competing to see who can give the most away. In Amazonian (or North American) societies, the institution of the chief played the same role on a political level: the position was so demanding, and so little rewarding, so hedged about by safeguards, that there was no way for power-hungry individuals to do much with it. Amazonians might not have literally whacked off the ruler's head every few years, but it's not an entirely inappropriate metaphor.

By these lights these were all, in a very real sense, anarchist societies. They were founded on an explicit rejection of the logic of the state and of the market.

They are, however, extremely imperfect ones. The most common criticism of Clastres is to ask how his Amazonians could really be organizing their societies against the emergence of something they have never actually experienced. A naive question, but it points to something equally naive in Clastres' own approach. Clastres manages to talk blithely about the uncompromised egalitarianism of the very same Amazonian societies, for instance, famous for their use of gang rape as a weapon to terrorize women who transgress proper gender roles. It's a blind spot so glaring one has to wonder how he could possibly miss out on it; especially considering it provides an answer to just that question. Perhaps Amazonian men understand what arbitrary, unquestionable power, backed by force, would be like because they themselves wield that sort of power over their wives and daughters. Perhaps for that very reason they would not like to see structures capable of inflicting it on them.

It's worth pointing out because Clastres is, in many ways, a naive romantic. Fom another perspective, though, there's no mystery here at all. After all, we are talking about the fact that most Amazonians don't want to give others the power to threaten them with physical injury if they don't do as they are told. Maybe we should better be asking what it says about ourselves that we feel this attitude needs any sort of explanation.

toward a theory of imaginary counterpower

This is what I mean by an alternative ethics, then. Anarchistic societies are no more unaware of human capacities for greed or vainglory than modern Americans are unaware of human capacities for envy, gluttony, or sloth; they would just find them equally unappealing as the basis for their civilization. In fact, they see these phenomena as moral dangers so dire they end up organizing much of their social life around containing them.

If this were a purely theoretical essay I would explain that all this suggests an interesting way of synthesizing theories of value and theories of resistance. For present purposes, suffice it to say that I think Mauss and Clastres have succeeded, somewhat despite themselves, in laying the groundwork for a theory of revolutionary counterpower.

I'm afraid this is a somewhat complicated argument. Let me take it one step at a time.

In typical revolutionary discourse a "counterpower" is a collection of social institutions set in opposition to the state and capital: from self-governing communities to radical labor unions to popular militias. Sometimes it is also referred to as an "anti-power." When such institutions maintain themselves in the face of the state, this is usually referred to as a "dual power" situation. By this definition most of human history is actually characterized by dual power situations, since few historical states had the means to root such institutions out, even assuming that they would have wanted to. But Mauss and Clastres' argument suggests something even more radical. It suggests that counterpower, at least in the most elementary sense, actually exists where the states and markets are not even present; that in such cases, rather than being embodied in popular institutions which pose themselves against the power of lords, or kings, or plutocrats, they are embodied in institutions which ensure such types of person never come about. What it is "counter" to, then, is a potential, a latent aspect, or dialectical possibility if you prefer, within the society itself.

This at least would help explain an otherwise peculiar fact; the way in which it is often particularly the egalitarian societies which are torn by terrible inner tensions, or at least, extreme forms of symbolic violence.

Of course, all societies are to some degree at war with themselves. There are always clashes between interests, factions, classes and the like; also, social systems are always based on the pursuit of different forms of value which pull people in different directions. In egalitarian societies, which tend to place an enormous emphasis on creating and maintaining communal consensus, this often appears to spark a kind of equally elaborate reaction formation, a spectral nightworld inhabited by monsters, witches or other creatures of horror. And it's the most peaceful societies which are also the most haunted, in their imaginative constructions of the cosmos, by constant specters of perennial war. The invisible worlds surrounding them are literally battlegrounds. It's as if the endless labor of achieving consensus masks a constant inner violence—or, it might perhaps be better to say, is in fact the process by which that inner violence is measured and contained—and it is precisely this, and the resulting tangle of moral contradiction, which is the prime font of social creativity. It's not these conflicting principles and contradictory impulses themselves which are the ultimate political reality, then; it's the regulatory process which mediates them.

Some examples might help here:

Case 1: The Piaroa, a highly egalitarian society living along tributaries of the Orinoco which ethnographer Joanna Overing herself describes as anarchists. They place enormous value on individual freedom and autonomy, and are quite self-conscious about the importance of ensuring that no one is ever at another person's orders, or the need to ensure no one gains such control over economic resources that they can use it to constrain others' freedom. Yet they also insist that Piaroa culture itself was the creation of an evil god, a two-headed cannibalistic buffoon. The Piaroa have developed a moral philosophy which defines the human condition as caught between a "world of the senses," of wild, pre-social desires, and a "world of thought." Growing up involves learning to control and channel in the former through thoughtful consideration for others, and the cultivation of a sense of humor; but this is made infinitely more difficult by the fact that all forms of technical knowledge, however necessary for life are, due to their origins, laced with elements of destructive madness. Similarly, while the Piaroa are famous for their peaceableness—murder is unheard of, the assumption being that anyone who killed another human being would be instantly consumed by pollution and die horribly—they inhabit a cosmos of endless invisible war, in which wizards are engaged in fending off the attacks of insane, predatory gods and all deaths are caused by spiritual murder and have to be avenged by the magical massacre of whole (distant, unknown) communities.

Case 2: The Tiv, another notoriously egalitarian society, make their homes along the Benue River in central Nigeria. Compared to the Piaroa, their domestic life is quite hierarchical: male elders tend to have many wives, and exchange with one another the rights to younger women's fertility; younger men are thus reduced to spending most of their lives chilling their heels as unmarried dependents in their fathers' compounds. In recent centuries the Tiv were never entirely insulated from the raids of slave traders; Tivland was also dotted with local markets; minor wars between clans were occasionally fought, though more often large disputes were mediated in large communal "moots." Still, there were no political institutions larger than the compound; in fact, anything that even began to look like a political institution was considered intrinsically suspect, or more precisely, seen as surrounded by an aura of occult horror. This was, as ethnographer Paul Bohannan succinctly put it, because of what was seen to be the nature of power: "men attain power by consuming the substance of others." Markets were protected, and market rules enforced by charms which embodied diseases and were said to be powered by human body parts and blood. Enterprising men who managed to patch together some sort of fame, wealth, or clientele were by definition witches. Their hearts were coated by a substance called *tsav*, which could only be augmented by the eating of human flesh. Most tried to avoid doing so, but a secret society of witches was said to exist which would slip bits of human flesh in their victims' food, thus incurring a "flesh debt" and unnatural cravings that would eventually drive those affected to consume their entire families. This imaginary society of witches was seen as the invisible government of the country. Power was thus institutionalized evil, and every generation, a witch-finding movement would arise to expose the culprits, thus, effectively, destroying any emerging structures of authority.

Case 3: Highland Madagascar, where I lived between 1989 and 1991, was a rather different place. The area had been the center of a Malagasy state—the Merina kingdom—since the early nineteenth century, and afterwards endured many years of harsh colonial rule. There was a market economy and, in theory, a central government—during the time I was there, largely dominated by what was called the "Merina bourgeoisie." In fact this government had effectively withdrawn from most of the countryside and rural communities were effectively governing themselves. In many ways these could also be considered anarchistic: most local decisions were made by consensus by informal bodies, leadership was looked on at best with suspicion, it was considered wrong for adults to be giving one another orders, especially on an ongoing basis; this was considered to make even institutions like wage labor inherently morally suspect. Or to be more precise, unmalagasy—this was how the French behaved, or wicked kings and slaveholders long ago. Society was overall remarkably peaceable. Yet once again it was surrounded by invisible warfare; just about everyone had access to dangerous medicine or spirits or was willing to let on they might; the night was haunted by witches who danced naked on tombs and rode men like horses; just about all sickness was due to envy, hatred, and magical attack. What's more, witchcraft bore a strange, ambivalent relation to national identity. While people made rhetorical reference to Malagasy as equal and united "like hairs on a head," ideals of economic equality were rarely, if ever, invoked; however, it was assumed that anyone who became too rich or powerful would be destroyed by witchcraft, and while witchcraft was the definition of evil, it was also seen as peculiarly Malagasy (charms were just charms but evil charms were called "Malagasy charms"). Insofar as rituals of moral solidarity did occur, and the ideal of equality was invoked, it was largely in the course of rituals held to suppress, expel, or destroy those witches who, perversely, were the twisted embodiment and practical enforcement of the egalitarian ethos of the society itself.

Note how in each case there's a striking contrast between the cosmological content, which is nothing if not tumultuous, and social process, which is all about mediation, arriving at consensus. None of these societies are entirely egalitarian: there are always certain key forms of dominance, at least of men over women, elders over juniors. The nature and intensity of these forms vary enormously: in Piaroa communities the hierarchies were so modest that Overing doubts one can really speak of "male dominance" at all (despite the fact that communal leaders are invariably male); the Tiv appear to be quite another story. Still, structural inequalities invariably exist, and as a result I think it is fair to say that these anarchies are not only imperfect, they contain with them the seeds of their own destruction. It is hardly a coincidence that when larger, more systematically violent forms of domination do emerge, they draw on precisely these idioms of age and gender to justify themselves.

Still, I think it would be a mistake to see the invisible violence and terror as simply a working out of the "internal contradictions" created by those forms of inequality. One could, perhaps, make the case that most real, tangible violence is. At least, it is a somewhat notorious thing that, in societies where the only notable inequalities are based in gender, the only murders one is likely to observe are men killing each other over women. Similarly, it does seem to be the case, generally speaking, that the more pronounced the differences between male and female roles in a society, the more physically violent it tends to be. But this hardly means that if all inequalities vanished, then everything, even the imagination, would become placid and untroubled. To some degree, I suspect all this turbulence stems from the very nature of the human condition. There would appear to be no society which does not see human life as fundamentally a problem. However much they might differ on what they deem the problem to be, at the very least, the existence of work, sex, and repro-duction are seen as fraught with all sorts of quan-daries; human desires are always fickle; and then there's the fact that we're all going to die. So there's a lot to be troubled by. None of these dilemmas are going to vanish if we eliminate structural inequalities (much though I think this would radically improve things in just about every other way). Indeed, the fantasy that it might, that the human condition, desire, mortality, can all be somehow resolved seems to be an especially dangerous one, an image of utopia which always seems to lurk somewhere behind the pretentions of Power and the state. Instead, as I've suggested, the spectral violence seems to emerge from the very tensions inherent in the project of main-taining an egalitarian society. Otherwise, one would at least imagine the Tiv imagination would be more tumultuous than the Piaroa.

That the state emerged from images of an impossible resolution of the human condition was Clastres' point as well. He argued that historically, the institution of the state could not have possibly emerged from the polit-ical institutions of anarchist societies, which were designed to ensure this never happened. Instead, it could only have been from religious institutions: he pointed to the Tupinamba prophets who led the whole population on a vast migration in search of a "land without evil." Of course, in later contexts, what Peter Lamborn Wilson calls "the Clastrian machine," that set of mechanisms which oppose the emergence of domination, what I'm calling the apparatus of counterpower, can itself become caught in such apocalyptic fantasies.

Now, at this point the reader may be objecting, "Sure, but what does any of this have to do with the kind of insurrectionary communities which revolutionary theorists are normally referring to when they use the word 'counterpower'?"

Here it might be useful to look at the difference between the first two cases and the third—because the Malagasy communities I knew in 1990 were living in something which in many ways resembled an insurrectionary situation. Between the nineteenth century and the twentieth, there had been a remarkable transformation of popular attitudes. Just about all reports from the last century insisted that, despite widespread resentment against the corrupt and often brutal Malagasy government, no one questioned the legitimacy of the monarchy itself, or particularly, their absolute personal loyalty to the Queen. Neither would anyone explicitly question the legitimacy of slavery. After the French conquest of the island in 1895, followed immediately by the abolition of both the monarchy and slavery, all this seems to have changed extremely quickly. Before a generation was out, one began to encounter the attitude that I found to be well-nigh universal in the countryside a hundred years later: slavery was evil, and monarchs were seen as inherently immoral because they treated others like slaves. In the end, all relations of command (military service, wage labor, forced labor) came to be fused together in people's minds as variations on slavery; the very institutions which had previously been seen as beyond challenge were now the definition of illegitimacy, and this, especially among those who had the least access to higher education and French Enlightenment ideas. Being "Malagasy" came to be defined as rejecting such foreign ways. If one combines this attitude with constant passive resistance to state institutions, and the elaboration of autonomous, and relatively egalitarian modes of self-government, one could see what happened as a revolution. After the financial crisis of the '80s, the state in much of the country effectively collapsed, or anyway devolved into a matter of hollow form without the backing of systematic coercion. Rural people carried on much as they had before, going to offices periodically to fill out forms even though they were no longer paying any real taxes, the government was hardly providing services, and in the event of theft or even murder, police would no longer come. If a revolution is a matter of people resisting some form of power identified as oppressive, identifying some key aspect of that power as the source of what is fundamentally objectionable about it, and then trying to get rid of one's oppressors in such a way as to try to eliminate that sort of power completely from daily life, then it is hard to deny that, in some sense, this was indeed a revolution. It might not have involved an actual uprising, but it was a revolution nonetheless.

How long it would last is another question; it was a very fragile, tenuous sort of freedom. Many such enclaves have collapsed—in Madagascar as elsewhere. Others endure; new ones are being created all the time. The contemporary world is riddled with such anarchic spaces, and the more successful they are, the less likely we are to hear about them. It's only if such a space breaks down into violence that there's any chance outsiders will even find out that it exists.

The puzzling question is how such profound changes in popular attitudes could happen so fast? The likely answer is that they really didn't; there were probably things going on even under the nineteenth-century kingdom of which foreign observers (even those long resident on the island) were simply unaware. But clearly, too, something about the imposition of colonial rule allowed for a rapid reshuffling of priorities. This, I would argue, is what the ongoing existence of deeply embedded forms of counterpower allows. A lot of the ideological work, in fact, of making a revolution was conducted precisely in the spectral nightworld of sorcerers and witches; in redefinitions of the moral implications of different forms of magical power. But this only underlines how these spectral zones are always the fulcrum of the moral imagination, a kind of creative reservoir, too, of potential revolutionary change. It's precisely from these invisible spaces—invisible, most of all, to power—whence the potential for insurrection, and the extraordinary social creativity that seems to emerge out of nowhere in revolutionary moments, actually comes.

To sum up the argument so far, then:

1) Counterpower is first and foremost rooted in the imagination; it emerges from the fact that all social systems are a tangle of contradictions, always to some degree at war with themselves. Or, more precisely, it is rooted in the relation between the practical imagination required to maintain a society based on consensus (as any society not based on violence must, ultimately, be)—the constant work of imaginative identification with others that makes understanding possible—and the spectral violence which appears to be its constant, perhaps inevitable corollary.

2) In egalitarian societies, counterpower might be said to be the predominant form of social power. It stands guard over what are seen as certain frightening possibilities within the society itself: notably against the emergence of systematic forms of political or economic dominance.

2a) Institutionally, counterpower takes the form of what we would call institutions of direct democracy, consensus and mediation; that is, ways of publicly negotiating and controlling that inevitable internal tumult and transforming it into those social states (or if you like, forms of value) that society sees as the most desirable: conviviality, unanimity, fertility, prosperity, beauty, however it may be framed.

3) In highly unequal societies, imaginative counterpower often defines itself against certain aspects of dominance that are seen as particularly obnoxious and can become an attempt to eliminate them from social relations completely. When it does, it becomes revolutionary.

    3a) Institutionally, as an imaginative well, it is responsible for the creation of new social forms, and the revalorization or transformation of old ones, and also,

4) in moments of radical transformation—revolutions in the old-fashioned sense—this is precisely what allows for the notorious popular ability to innovate entirely new politics, economic, and social forms. Hence, it is the root of what Antonio Negri has called "constituent power," the power to create constitutions.

Most modern constitutional orders see themselves as having been created by rebellions: the American revolution, the French revolution, and so on. This has, of course, not always been the case. But this leads to a very important question, because any really politically engaged anthropology will have to start by seriously confronting the question of what, if anything, really divides what we like to call the "modern" world from the rest of human history, to which folks like the Piaroa, Tiv or Malagasy are normally relegated. This is as one might imagine a pretty vexed question but I am afraid it can't be avoided, since otherwise, many readers might not be convinced there's any reason to have an anarchist anthropology to begin with.

Blowing Up Walls

As I remarked, an anarchist anthropology doesn't really exist. There are only fragments. In the first part of this essay I tried to gather some of them, and to look for common themes; in this part I want to go further, and imagine a body of social theory that might exist at some time in the future.

obvious objections

Before being able to do so I really do need to address the usual objection to any project of this nature: that the study of actually-existing anarchist societies is simply irrelevant to the modern world. After all, aren't we just talking about a bunch of primitives?

For anarchists who do know something about anthropology, the arguments are all too familiar. A typical exchange goes something like this:

> **Skeptic:** Well, I might take this whole anarchism idea more seriously if you could give me some reason to think it would work. Can you name me a single viable example of a society which has existed without a government?
>
> **Anarchist:** Sure. There have been thousands. I could name a dozen just off the top of my head: the Bororo, the Baining, the Onondaga, the Wintu, the Ema, the Tallensi, the Vezo...
>
> **Skeptic:** But those are all a bunch of primitives! I'm talking about anarchism in a modern, technological society.

Anarchist: Okay, then. There have been all sorts of successful experiments: experiments with worker's self-management, like Mondragon; economic projects based on the idea of the gift economy, like Linux; all sorts of political organizations based on consensus and direct democracy...

Skeptic: Sure, sure, but these are small, isolated examples. I'm talking about whole societies.

Anarchist: Well, it's not like people haven't tried. Look at the Paris Commune, the revolution in Republican Spain...

Skeptic: Yeah, and look what happened to those guys! They all got killed!

The dice are loaded. You can't win. Because when the skeptic says "society," what he really means is "state," even "nation-state." Since no one is going to produce an example of an anarchist state—that would be a contradiction in terms—what we're really being asked for is an example of a modern nation-state with the government somehow plucked away: a situation in which the government of Canada, to take a random example, has been overthrown, or for some reason abolished itself, and no new one has taken its place but instead all former Canadian citizens begin to organize themselves into libertarian collectives. Obviously this would never be allowed to happen. In the past, whenever it even looked like it might—here, the Paris commune and Spanish civil war are excellent examples—the politicians running pretty much every state in the vicinity have been willing to put their differences on hold until those trying to bring such a situation about had been rounded up and shot.

There is a way out, which is to accept that anarchist forms of organization would not look anything like a state. That they would involve an endless variety of communities, associations, networks, projects, on every conceivable scale, over-lapping and intersecting in any way we could imagine, and possibly many that we can't. Some would be quite local, others global. Perhaps all they would have in common is that none would involve anyone showing up with weapons and telling everyone else to shut up and do what they were told. And that, since anarchists are not actually trying to seize power within any national territory, the process of one system replacing the other will not take the form of some sudden revo-lutionary cataclysm—the storming of a Bastille, the seizing of a Winter Palace—but will necessarily be gradual, the creation of alternative forms of organiza-tion on a world scale, new forms of communication, new, less alienated ways of organizing life, which will, eventually, make currently existing forms of power seem stupid and beside the point. That in turn would mean that there are endless examples of viable anar-chism: pretty much any form of organization would count as one, so long as it was not imposed by some higher authority, from a klezmer band to the interna-tional postal service.

Unfortunately, this kind of argument does not seem to satisfy most skeptics. They want "societies." So one is reduced to scouring the historical and ethnographic record for entities that look like a nation-state (one people, speaking a common language, living within a bounded territory, acknowledging a common set of legal principles...), but which lack a state apparatus (which, following Weber, one can define roughly as: a group of people who claim that, at least when they are around and in their official capacity, they are the only ones with the right to act violently). These, too, one can find, if one is willing to look at relatively small communities far away in time or space. But then one is told they don't count for just this reason.

So we're back to the original problem. There is assumed to be an absolute rupture between the world we live in, and the world inhabited by anyone who might be characterized as "primitive," "tribal," or even as "peasants." Anthropologists are not to blame here: we have been trying for decades now to convince the public that there's no such thing as a "primitive," that "simple societies" are not really all that simple, that no one ever existed in timeless isolation, that it makes no sense to speak of some social systems as more or less evolved; but so far, we've made very little headway. It is almost impossible to convince the average American that a bunch of Amazonians could possibly have anything to teach them—other than, conceivably, that we should all abandon modern civilization and go live in Amazonia—and this because they are assumed to live in an absolutely different world. Which is, oddly enough, again because of the way we are used to thinking about revolutions.

Let me take up the argument I began to sketch out in the last section and try to explain why I think this is true:

a fairly brief manifesto
concerning the concept of revolution:

The term "revolution" has been so relentlessly cheapened in common usage that it can mean almost anything. We have revolutions every week now: banking revolutions, cybernetic revolutions, medical revolutions, an internet revolution every time someone invents some clever new piece of software.

This kind of rhetoric is only possible because the commonplace definition of revolution has always implied something in the nature of a paradigm shift: a clear break, a fundamental rupture in the nature of social reality after which everything works differently, and previous categories no longer apply. It is this which makes it possible to, say, claim that the modern world is derived from two "revolutions": the French revolution and the Industrial revolution, despite the fact that the two had almost nothing else in common other than seeming to mark a break with all that came before. One odd result is that, as Ellen Meskins Wood has noted, we are in the habit of discussing what we call "modernity" as if it involved a combination of English laissez faire economics, and French Republican government, despite the fact that the two never really occurred together: the industrial revolution happened under a bizarre, antiquated, still largely medieval English constitution, and nineteenth-century France was anything but laissez faire.

(The one-time appeal of the Russian revolution for the "developing world" seems to derive from the fact it's the one example where both sorts of revolution did seem to coincide: a seizure of

national power which then led to rapid industrial-
ization. As a result almost every twentieth-century
government in the global south determined to play
economic catch-up with the industrial powers had
also to claim to be a revolutionary regime.)

If there is one logical error underlying all this,
it rests on imagining that social or even technological change takes the same form of what Thomas
Kuhn has called "the structure of scientific revolutions." Kuhn is referring to events like the shift
from a Newtonian to Einsteinian universe:
suddenly there is an intellectual breakthrough and
afterwards, the universe is different. Applied to
anything other than scientific revolutions, it
implies that the world really was equivalent to our
knowledge of it, and the moment we change the
principles on which our knowledge is based, reality
changes too. This is just the sort of basic intellectual mistake developmental psychologists say we're
supposed to get over in early childhood, but it
seems few of us really do.

In fact, the world is under no obligation to live
up to our expectations, and insofar as "reality"
refers to anything, it refers to precisely that which
can never be entirely encompassed by our imaginative constructions. Totalities, in particular, are
always creatures of the imagination. Nations, societies, ideologies, closed systems... none of these
really exist. Reality is always infinitely messier than
that—even if the belief that they exist is an unde-
niable social force. For one thing, the habit of
thought which defines the world, or society, as a
totalizing system (in which every element takes on
its significance only in relation to the others) tends
to lead almost inevitably to a view of revolutions as

cataclysmic ruptures. Since, after all, how else could one totalizing system be replaced by a completely different one than by a cataclysmic rupture? Human history thus becomes a series of revolutions: the Neolithic revolution, the Industrial revolution, the Information revolution, etc., and the political dream becomes to somehow take control of the process; to get to the point where we can cause a rupture of this sort, a momentous breakthrough that will not just happen but result directly from some kind of collective will. "The revolution," properly speaking.

If so it's not surprising that the moment radical thinkers felt they had to give up this dream, their first reaction was to redouble their efforts to identify revolutions happening anyway, to the point where in the eyes of someone like Paul Virilio, rupture is our permanent state of being, or for someone like Jean Baudrillard, the world now changes completely every couple years, whenever he gets a new idea.

This is not an appeal for a flat-out rejection of such imaginary totalities—even assuming this were possible, which it probably isn't, since they are probably a necessary tool of human thought. It is an appeal to always bear in mind that they are just that: tools of thought. For instance, it is indeed a very good thing to be able to ask "after the revolution, how will we organize mass transportation?," "who will fund scientific research?," or even, "after the revolution, do you think there will still be fashion magazines?" The phrase is a useful mental hinge; even if we also recognize that in reality, unless we are willing to massacre thousands of people (and probably even then), the revolution will almost certainly not be quite such a clean break as such a phrase implies.

What will it be, then? I have already made some suggestions. A revolution on a world scale will take a very long time. But it is also possible to recognize that it is already starting to happen. The easiest way to get our minds around it is to stop thinking about revolution as a thing—"the" revolution, the great cataclysmic break—and instead ask "what is revolutionary action?" We could then suggest: revolutionary action is any collective action which rejects, and therefore confronts, some form of power or domination and in doing so, reconstitutes social relations—even within the collectivity—in that light. Revolutionary action does not necessarily have to aim to topple governments. Attempts to create autonomous communities in the face of power (using Castoriadis' definition here: ones that constitute themselves, collectively make their own rules or principles of operation, and continually reexamine them), would, for instance, be almost by definition revolutionary acts. And history shows us that the continual accumulation of such acts can change (almost) everything.

I'm hardly the first to have made an argument like this—some such vision follows almost necessarily once one is no longer thinking in terms of the framework of the state and seizure of state power. What I want to emphasize here is what this means for how we look at history.

a thought experiment, or, blowing up walls

What I am proposing, essentially, is that we engage in a kind of thought experiment. What if, as a recent title put it, "we have never been modern"? What if there never was any fundamental break, and therefore, we are not living in a fundamentally different moral, social, or political universe than the Piaroa or Tiv or rural Malagasy?

There are a million different ways to define "modernity." According to some it mainly has to do with science and technology, for others it's a matter of individualism; others, capitalism, or bureaucratic rationality, or alienation, or an ideal of freedom of one sort or another. However they define it, almost everyone agrees that at somewhere in the sixteenth, or seventeenth, or eighteenth centuries, a Great Transformation occurred, that it occurred in Western Europe and its settler colonies, and that because of it, we became "modern." And that once we did, we became a fundamentally different sort of creature than anything that had come before.

But what if we kicked this whole apparatus away? What if we blew up the wall? What if we accepted that the people who Columbus or Vasco da Gama "discovered" on their expeditions were just us? Or certainly, just as much "us" as Columbus and Vasco da Gama ever were?

I'm not arguing that nothing important has changed over the last five hundred years, any more than I'm arguing that cultural differences are unimportant. In one sense everyone, every community, every individual for that matter, lives in their own unique universe. By "blowing up walls," I mean most of all, blowing up the arrogant, unreflecting assumptions which tell us we have nothing in common with 98% of people who ever lived, so we don't really have to think about them. Since, after all, if you assume the fundamental break, the only theoretical question you can ask is some variation on "what makes us so special?" Once we get rid of those assumptions, decide to at least entertain the notion we aren't quite so special as we might like to think, we can also begin to think about what really has changed and what hasn't.

An example:

There has long been a related debate over what particular advantage "the West," as Western Europe and its settler colonies have liked to call themselves, had over the rest of the world that allowed them to conquer so much of it in the four hundred years between 1500 and 1900. Was it a more efficient economic system? A superior military tradition? Did it have to do with Christianity, or Protestantism, or a spirit of rationalistic inquiry? Was it simply a matter of technology? Or did it have to do with more individualistic family arrangements? Some combination of all these factors? To a large extent, Western historical sociology has been dedicated to solving this problem. It is a sign of how deeply embedded the assumptions are that it is only quite recently that scholars have come to even suggest that perhaps, Western Europe didn't really have any fundamental advantage at all. That European technology, economic and social arrangements, state organization, and the rest in 1450 were in no way more "advanced" than what prevailed in Egypt, or Bengal, or Fujian, or most any other urbanized part of the Old World at the time. Europe might have been ahead in some areas (e.g., techniques of naval warfare, certain forms of banking), but lagged significantly behind in others (astronomy, jurisprudence, agricultural technology, techniques of land warfare). Perhaps there was no mysterious advantage. Perhaps what happened was just a coincidence. Western Europe happened to be located in that part of the Old World where it was easiest to sail to the New; those who first did so had the incredible luck to discover lands full of enormous wealth, populated by defenseless stone-age peoples who conveniently began dying almost the moment they arrived; the resultant windfall, and the demographic advantage from having lands to siphon off excess population was more than enough to account for the European powers' later successes. It was then possible to shut down the (far more efficient) Indian cloth industry and create the space for an industrial revolution, and generally ravage and dominate Asia to such an extent that in technological terms—particularly industrial and military technology—it fell increasingly behind.

A number of authors (Blaut, Goody, Pommeranz, Gunder Frank) have been making some variation of this argument in recent years. It is at root a moral argument, an attack on Western arrogance. As such it is extremely important. The only problem with it, in moral terms, is that it tends to confuse means and inclination. That is, it rests on the assumption that Western historians were right to assume that whatever it was that made it possible for Europeans to dispossess, abduct, enslave, and exterminate millions of other human beings, it was a mark of superiority and that therefore, whatever it was, it would be insulting to non-Europeans to suggest they didn't have it too. It seems to me that it is far more insulting to suggest anyone would ever have behaved like Europeans of the sixteenth or seventeenth centuries—e.g., depopulating large portions of the Andes or central Mexico by working millions to death in the mines, or kidnapping a significant chunk of the population of Africa to work to death on sugar plantations—unless one has some actual evidence to suggest they were so genocidally inclined. In fact there appear to have been plenty of examples of people in a position to wreak similar havoc on a world scale—say, the Ming dynasty in the fifteenth century—but who didn't, not so much because they scrupled to, so much as because it would never have occurred to them to act this way to begin with.

In the end it all turns, oddly enough, on how one chooses to define capitalism. Almost all the authors cited above tend to see capitalism as yet another accomplishment which Westerners arrogantly assume they invented themselves, and therefore define it (as capitalists do) as largely a matter of commerce and financial instruments. But that willingness to put considerations of profit above any human concern which drove Europeans to depopulate whole regions of the world in order to place the maximum amount of silver or sugar on the market was certainly something else. It seems to me it deserves a name of its own. For this reason it seems better to me to continue to define capi-

talism as its opponents prefer, as founded on the
connection between a wage system and a principle
of the never-ending pursuit of profit for its own
sake. This in turn makes it possible to argue this
was a strange perversion of normal commercial
logic which happened to take hold in one, previously rather barbarous, corner of the world and
encouraged the inhabitants to engage in what
might otherwise have been considered unspeakable
forms of behavior. Again, all this does not necessarily mean that one has to agree with the premise
that once capitalism came into existence, it
instantly became a totalizing system and that from
that moment, everything else that happened can
only be understood in relation to it. But it suggests
one of the axes on which one can begin to think
about what really is different nowadays.

Let us imagine, then, that the West, however
defined, was nothing special, and further, that there
has been no one fundamental break in human history.
No one can deny there have been massive quantitative
changes: the amount of energy consumed, the speed at
which humans can travel, the number of books
produced and read, all these numbers have been rising
exponentially. But let us imagine for the sake of argument that these quantitative changes do not, in themselves, necessarily imply a change in quality: we are
not living in a fundamentally different sort of society
than has ever existed before, we are not living in a
fundamentally different sort of time, the existence of
factories or microchips do not mean political or social
possibilities have changed in their basic nature: Or, to

be more precise, the West might have introduced some new possibilities, but it hasn't canceled any of the old ones out.

The first thing one discovers when one tries to think this way is that it is extremely difficult to do so. One has to cut past the endless host of intellectual tricks and gimmicks that create the wall of distance around "modern" societies. Let me give just one example. It is common to distinguish between what are called "kinship-based societies" and modern ones, which are supposed to be based on impersonal institutions like the market or the state. The societies traditionally studied by anthropologists have kinship systems. They are organized into descent groups—lineages, or clans, or moieties, or ramages—which trace descent to common ancestors, live mainly on ancestral territories, are seen as consisting of similar "kinds" of people—an idea usually expressed through physical idioms of common flesh, or bone, or blood, or skin. Often kinship systems become a basis of social inequality as some groups are seen as higher than others, as for example in caste systems; always, kinship establishes the terms for sex and marriage and the passing of property over the generations.

The term "kin-based" is often used the way people used to use the word "primitive"; these are exotic societies which are in no way like our own. (That's why it is assumed we need anthropology to study them; entirely different disciplines, like sociology and economics, are assumed to be required to study modern ones.) But then the exact same people who make this argument will usually take it for granted that the main social problems in our own, "modern" society (or "postmodern": for present purposes it's exactly the same thing) revolve around race, class, and gender. In other words, precisely from the nature of our kinship system.

After all, what does it mean to say most Americans see the world as divided into "races"? It means they believe that it is divided into groups which are presumed to share a common descent and geographical origin, who for this reason are seen as different "kinds" of people, that this idea is usually expressed through physical idioms of blood and skin, and that the resulting system regulates sex, marriage, and the inheritance of property and therefore creates and maintains social inequalities. We are talking about something very much like a classic clan system, except on a global scale. One might object that there is a lot of interracial marriage going on, and even more inter-racial sex, but then, this is only what we should expect. Statistical studies always reveal that, even in "tradi-tional" societies like the Nambikwara or Arapesh, at least 5-10% of young people marry someone they're not supposed to. Statistically, the phenomena are of about equal significance. Social class is slightly more complicated, since the groups are less clearly bounded. Still, the difference between a ruling class and a collection of people who happen to have done well is, precisely, kinship: the ability to marry one's children off appropriately, and pass one's advantages on to one's descendants. People marry across class lines too, but rarely very far; and while most Americans seem to be under the impression that this is a country of considerable class mobility, when asked to adduce examples all they can usually come up with is a handful of rags to riches stories. It is almost impossible to find an example of an American who was born rich and ended up a penniless ward of the state. So all we are really dealing with then is the fact, familiar to anyone who's studied history, that ruling elites (unless polygamous) are never able to reproduce themselves demographically, and therefore always need some way to recruit new blood (and if they are polygamous, of course, that itself becomes a mode of social mobility).

Gender relations are of course the very fabric of kinship.

what would it take to knock down these walls?

I'd say a lot. Too many people have too much invested in maintaining them. This includes anarchists, incidentally. At least in the United States, the anarchists who do take anthropology the most seriously are the Primitivists, a small but very vocal faction who argue that the only way to get humanity back on track is to shuck off modernity entirely. Inspired by Marshall Sahlins' essay "The Original Affluent Society," they propose that there was a time when alienation and inequality did not exist, when everyone was a hunter-gathering anarchist, and that therefore real liberation can only come if we abandon "civilization" and return to the Upper Paleolithic, or at least the early Iron Age. In fact we know almost nothing about life in the Paleolithic, other than the sort of thing that can be gleaned from studying very old skulls (i.e., in the Paleolithic people had much better teeth; they also died much more frequently from traumatic head wounds). But what we see in the more recent ethnographic record is endless variety. There were hunter-gatherer societies with nobles and slaves, there are agrarian societies that are fiercely egalitarian. Even in Clastres' favored stomping grounds in Amazonia, one finds some groups who can justly be described as anarchists, like the Piaroa, living alongside others (say, the warlike Sherente) who are clearly anything but. And "societies" are constantly reforming, skipping back and forth between what we think of as different evolutionary stages.

I do not think we're losing much if we admit that humans never really lived in the garden of Eden. Knocking the walls down can allow us to see this history as a resource to us in much more interesting ways. Because it works both ways. Not only do we, in industrial societies, still have kinship (and cosmologies); other societies have social movements and revolutions. Which means, among other things, that radical theorists no longer have to pore endlessly over the same scant two hundred years of revolutionary history.

Between the sixteenth and nineteenth centuries the west coast of Madagascar was divided into a series of related kingdoms under the Maroansetra dynasty. Their subjects were collectively known as the Sakalava. In northwest Madagascar there is now an "ethnic group" ensconced in a somewhat difficult, hilly back country referred to as the Tsimihety. The word literally means "those who do not cut their hair." This refers to a Sakalava custom: when a king died, his male subjects were all expected to crop off their hair as a sign of mourning. The Tsimihety were those who refused, and hence rejected the authority of the Sakalava monarchy; to this day they are marked by resolutely egalitarian social organization and practices. They are, in other words, the anarchists of northwest Madagascar. To this day they have maintained a reputation as masters of evasion: under the French, administrators would complain that they could send delegations to arrange for labor to build a road near a Tsimihety village, negotiate the terms with apparently cooperative elders, and return with the equipment a week later only to discover the village entirely abandoned—every single inhabitant had moved in with some relative in another part of the country.

What especially interests me here is the principle of "ethnogenesis," as it's called nowadays. The Tsimihety are now considered a *foko*—a people or ethnic group— but their identity emerged as a political project. The desire to live free of Sakalava domination was translated into a desire—one which came to suffuse all social institutions from village assemblies to mortuary ritual—to live in a society free of markers of hierarchy. This then became institutionalized as a way of life of a community living together, which then in turn came to be thought of as a particular "kind" of people, an ethnic group—people who also, since they tend to intermarry, come to be seen as united by common ancestry. It is easier to see this happening in Madagascar where everyone pretty much speaks the same language. But I doubt it is that unusual. The ethnogenesis literature is a fairly new one, but it is becoming increasingly clear that most of human history was characterized by continual social change. Rather than timeless groups living for thousands of years in their ancestral territories, new groups were being created, and old ones dissolving, all the time. Many of what we have come to think of as tribes, or nations, or ethnic groups were originally collective projects of some sort. In the Tsimihety case we are talking about a revolutionary project, at least revolutionary in that sense I have been developing here: a conscious rejection of certain forms of overarching political power which also causes people to rethink and reorganize the way they deal with one another on an everyday basis. Most are not. Some are egalitarian, others are about promoting a certain vision of authority or hierarchy. Still, one is dealing with something very much along the lines of what we'd think of as a social movement; it is just that, in the absence of broadsides, rallies and manifestos, the media through which one can create and demand new forms of (what we'd call) social, economic or political life, to pursue different forms of value, were different: one had to work through literally or figuratively sculpting flesh, through music and ritual, food and clothing, and ways of disposing of the dead. But in part as a result, over time, what were once projects become identities, even ones continuous with nature. They ossify and harden into self-evident truths or collective properties.

A whole discipline could no doubt be invented to understand precisely how this happens: a process in only some ways analogous to Weber's "routinization of charisma," full of strategies, reversals, diversions of energy... Social fields which are, in their essence, arenas for the recognition of certain forms of value can become borders to be defended; representations or media of value become numinous powers in themselves; creation slips into commemoration; the ossified remains of liberatory movements can end up, under the grip of states, transformed into what we call "nationalisms" which are either mobilized to rally support for the state machinery or become the basis for new social movements opposed to them.

The critical thing here, it seems to me, is that this petrification does not only apply to social projects. It can also happen to the states themselves. This is a phenomenon theorists of social struggle have rarely fully appreciated.

When the French colonial administration established itself in Madagascar it duly began dividing the population up into a series of "tribes": Merina, Betsileo, Bara, Sakalava, Vezo, Tsimihety, etc. Since there are few clear distinctions of language, it is easier here, than in most places, to discern some of the principles by which these divisions came about. Some are political. The Sakalava are noted subjects of the Maroantsetra dynasty (which created at least three kingdoms along the West coast). The Tsimihety are those who refused allegiance. Those called the "Merina" are those highland people originally united by allegiance to a king named Andrianampoinimerina; subjects of other highland kingdoms to the south, who the Merina conquered almost immediately thereafter, are referred to collectively as Betsileo.

Some names have to do with where people live or how they make a living: the Tanala are "forest people" on the east coast; on the west coast, the Mikea are hunters and foragers and the Vezo, fisherfolk. But even here there are usually political elements: the Vezo lived alongside the Sakalava monarchies but like the Tsimihety, they managed to remain independent of them because, as legend has it, whenever they learned royal representatives were on the way to visit them, they would all get in their canoes and wait offshore until they went away. Those fishing villages that did succumb became Sakalava, not Vezo.

The Merina, Sakalava, and Betsileo are by far the most numerous however. So most Malagasy, then, are defined, not exactly by their political loyalties, but by the loyalties their ancestors had sometime around 1775 or 1800. The interesting thing is what happened to these identities once the kings were no longer around. Here the Merina and Betsileo seem to represent two opposite possibilities.

Many of these ancient kingdoms were little more than institutionalized extortion systems; insofar as ordinary folk actually participated in royal politics, it was through ritual labor: building royal palaces and tombs, for example, in which each clan was usually assigned some very specific honorific role. Within the Merina kingdom this system ended up being so thoroughly abused that by the time the French arrived, it had been almost entirely discredited and royal rule became, as I mentioned, identified with slavery and forced labor; as a result, the "Merina" now mainly exist on paper. One never hears anyone in the countryside referring to themselves that way except perhaps in essays they have to write in school. The Sakalava are quite another story. Sakalava is still very much a living identity on the West coast, and it continues to mean, followers of the Maroantsetra dynasty. But for the last hundred and fifty years or so, the primary loyalties of most Sakalava have been to the members of this dynasty who are dead. While living royalty are largely ignored, the ancient kings' tombs are still continually rebuilt and redecorated in vast communal projects and this is what being Sakalava is seen largely to be about. And dead kings still make their wishes known—through spirit mediums who are usually elderly women of commoner descent.

In many other parts of Madagascar as well, it often seems that no one really takes on their full authority until they are dead. So perhaps the Sakalava case is not that extraordinary. But it reveals one very common way of avoiding the direct effects of power: if one cannot simply step out of its path, like the Vezo or Tsimihety, one can, as it were, try to fossilize it. In the Sakalava case the ossification of the state is quite literal: the kings who are still worshipped take the physical form of royal relics, they are literally teeth and bones. But this approach is probably far more commonplace than we would be given to suspect.

Kajsia Eckholm for example has recently made the intriguing suggestion that the kind of divine kingship Sir James Frazer wrote about in *The Golden Bough*, in which kings were hedged about with endless ritual and taboo (not to touch the earth, not to see the sun...), was not, as we normally assume, an archaic form of kingship, but in most cases, a very late one.

She gives the example of the Kongo monarchy, which when the Portugese first showed up in the late fifteenth century doesn't seem to have been particularly more ritualized than the monarchy in Portugal or Spain at the same time. There was a certain amount of court ceremonial, but nothing that got in the way of governing. It was only later, as the kingdom collapsed into civil war and broke into tinier and tinier fragments, that its rulers became increasingly sacred beings. Elaborate rituals were created, restrictions multiplied, until by the end we read about "kings" who were confined to small buildings, or literally castrated on ascending the throne. As a result they ruled very little; most BaKongo had in fact passed to a largely self-governing system, though also a very tumultuous one, caught in the throes of the slave-trade.

Is any of this relevant to contemporary concerns? Very much so, it seems to me. Autonomist thinkers in Italy have, over the last couple decades, developed a theory of what they call revolutionary "exodus." It is inspired in part by particularly Italian conditions—the broad refusal of factory work among young people, the flourishing of squats and occupied "social centers" in so many Italian cities... But in all this Italy seems to have acted as a kind of laboratory for future social movements, anticipating trends that are now beginning to happen on a global scale.

The theory of exodus proposes that the most effective way of opposing capitalism and the liberal state is not through direct confrontation but by means of what Paolo Virno has called "engaged withdrawal," mass defection by those wishing to create new forms of community. One need only glance at the historical record to confirm that most successful forms of popular resistance have taken precisely this form. They have not involved challenging power head on (this usually leads to being slaughtered, or if not, turning into some—often even uglier—variant of the very thing one first challenged) but from one or another strategy of slipping away from its grasp, from flight, desertion, the founding of new communities. One Autonomist historian, Yann Moulier Boutang, has even argued that the history of capitalism has been a series of attempts to solve the problem of worker mobility—hence the endless elaboration of institutions like indenture, slavery, coolie systems, contract workers, guest workers, innumerable forms of border control—since, if the system ever really came close to its own fantasy version of itself, in which workers were free to hire on and quit their work wherever and whenever they wanted, the entire system would collapse. It's for precisely this reason that the one most consistent demand put forward by the radical elements in the globalization movement—from the Italian Autonomists to North American anarchists—has always been global freedom of movement, "real globalization," the destruction of borders, a general tearing down of walls.

The kind of tearing down of conceptual walls I've been proposing here makes it possible for us not only to confirm the importance of defection, it promises an infinitely richer conception of how alternative forms of revolutionary action might work. This is a history which has largely yet to be written, but there are glimmerings. Peter Lamborn Wilson has produced the brightest of these, in a series of essays which include reflections, on, among other things, the collapse of the Hopewell and Mississippian cultures through much of eastern North America. These were societies apparently dominated by priestly elites, caste-based social structures, and human sacrifice—which mysteriously disappeared, being replaced by far more egalitarian hunter/gathering or horticultural societies. He suggests, interestingly enough, that the famous Native American identification with nature might not really have been a reaction to European values, but to a dialectical possibility within their own societies from which they had quite consciously run away. The story continues through the defection of the Jamestown settlers, a collection of servants abandoned in the first North American colony in Virginia by their gentleman patrons, who apparently ended up becoming Indians, to an endless series of "pirate utopias," in which British renegades teamed up with Muslim corsairs, or joined native communities from Hispaniola to Madagascar, hidden "triracial" republics founded by escaped slaves at the margins of European settlements, Antinomians, and other little-known libertarian enclaves that riddled the continent even before the Shakers and Fourierists and all the better-known nineteenth-century "intentional communities."

Most of these little utopias were even more marginal than the Vezo or Tsimihety were in Madagascar; all of them were eventually gobbled up. Which leads to the question of how to neutralize the

state apparatus itself, in the absence of a politics of
direct confrontation. No doubt some states and corporate elites will collapse of their own dead weight; a few
already have; but it's hard to imagine a scenario in
which they all will. Here, the Sakalava and BaKongo
might be able to provide us some useful suggestions.
What cannot be destroyed can, nonetheless, be
diverted, frozen, transformed, and gradually deprived
of its substance—which in the case of states, is ultimately their capacity to inspire terror. What would
this mean under contemporary conditions? It's not
entirely clear. Perhaps existing state apparati will gradually be reduced to window-dressing as the substance
is pulled out of them from above and below: i.e., both
from the growth of international institutions, and
from devolution to local and regional forms of self-
governance. Perhaps government by media spectacle
will devolve into spectacle pure and simple (somewhat
along the lines of what Paul Lafargue, Marx's West
Indian son-in-law and author of *The Right to Be Lazy*,
implied when he suggested that after the revolution,
politicians would still be able to fulfill a useful social
function in the entertainment industry). More likely it
will happen in ways we cannot even anticipate. But no
doubt there are ways in which it is happening already.
As Neoliberal states move towards new forms of
feudalism, concentrating their guns increasingly
around gated communities, insurrectionary spaces
open up that we don't even know about. The Merina
rice farmers described in the last section understand
what many would-be revolutionaries do not: that there
are times when the stupidest thing one could possibly

do is raise a red or black flag and issue defiant declarations. Sometimes the sensible thing is just to pretend nothing has changed, allow official state representatives to keep their dignity, even show up at their offices and fill out a form now and then, but otherwise, ignore them.

Tenets of a Non-existent Science

Let me outline a few of the areas of theory an anarchist anthropology might wish to explore:

1) A THEORY OF THE STATE

States have a peculiar dual character. They are at the same time forms of institutionalized raiding or extortion, and utopian projects. The first certainly reflects the way states are actually experienced, by any communities that retain some degree of autonomy; the second however is how they tend to appear in the written record.

In one sense states are the "imaginary totality" par excellence, and much of the confusion entailed in theories of the state historically lies in an inability or unwillingness to recognize this. For the most part, states were ideas, ways of imagining social order as something one could get a grip on, models of control. This is why the first known works of social theory, whether from Persia, or China, or ancient Greece, were always framed as theories of statecraft. This has had two disastrous effects. One is to give utopianism a bad name. (The word "utopia" first calls to mind the image of an ideal city, usually, with perfect geometry—the image seems to harken back originally to the royal military camp: a geometrical space which is entirely the emanation of a single, individual will, a fantasy of total control.) All this has had dire political consequences, to say the least. The second is that we tend to assume that states, and social order, even societies, largely correspond. In other words, we have a tendency to take the most grandiose, even paranoid, claims of world-rulers seriously, assuming that whatever cosmological projects they claimed to be pursuing actually did correspond, at least roughly, to something on the ground. Whereas it is likely that in many such cases, these claims ordinarily only applied fully within a few dozen yards of the monarch in any direction, and most subjects were much more likely to see ruling elites, on a day-to-day basis, as something much along the lines of predatory raiders.

An adequate theory of states would then have to begin by distinguishing in each case between the relevant ideal of rulership (which can be almost anything, a need to enforce military style discipline, the ability to provide perfect theatrical representation of gracious living which will inspire others, the need to provide the gods with endless human hearts to fend off the apocalypse...), and the mechanics of rule, without assuming that there is necessarily all that much correspondence between them. (There might be. But this has to be empirically established.) For example: much of the mythology of "the West" goes back to Herodotus' description of an epochal clash between the Persian Empire, based on an ideal of obedience and absolute power, and the Greek cities of Athens and Sparta, based on ideals of civic autonomy, freedom and equality. It's not that these ideas—especially their vivid representations in poets like Aeschylus or historians like Herodotus—are not important. One could not possibly understand Western history without them. But their very importance and vividness long blinded historians to what is becoming the increasingly clear reality: that whatever its ideals, the Achmaenid Empire was a pretty light touch when it came to the day-to-day control of its subjects' lives, particularly in comparison with the degree of control exercised by Athenians over their slaves or Spartans over the overwhelming majority of the Laconian population, who were helots. Whatever the ideals, the reality, for most people involved, was much the other way around.

One of the most striking discoveries of evolutionary anthropology has been that it is perfectly possible to have kings and nobles and all the exterior trappings of monarchy without having a state in the mechanical sense at all. One should think this might be of some interest to all those political philosophers who spill so much ink arguing about theories of "sovereignty"—since it suggests that most sovereigns were not heads of state and that their favorite technical term actually is built on a near-impossible ideal, in which royal power actually does manage to translate its cosmological pretensions into genuine bureaucratic control of a given territorial population. (Something like this started happening in Western Europe in the sixteenth and seventeenth centuries, but almost as soon as it did, the sovereign's personal power was replaced by a fictive person called "the people," allowing the bureaucracy to take over almost entirely.) But so far as I'm aware, political philosophers have as yet had nothing to say on the subject. I suspect this is largely due to an extremely poor choice of terms. Evolutionary anthropologists refer to kingdoms which lack full-fledged coercive bureaucracies as "chiefdoms," a term which evokes images more of Geronimo or Sitting Bull than Solomon, Louis the Pious, or the Yellow Emperor. And of course the evolutionist framework itself ensures that such structures are seen as something which immediately precedes the emergence of the state, not an alternative form, or even something a state can turn into. To clarify all this would be a major historical project.

2) A THEORY OF POLITICAL ENTITIES THAT ARE NOT STATES

So that's one project: to reanalyze the state as a relation between a utopian imaginary, and a messy reality involving strategies of flight and evasion, predatory elites, and a mechanics of regulation and control.

All this highlights the pressing need for another project: one which will ask, If many political entities we are used to seeing as states, at least in any Weberian sense, are not, then what are they? And what does that imply about political possibilities?

In a way it's kind of amazing that such a theoretical literature doesn't already exist. It's yet another sign, I guess, of how hard it is for us to think outside the statist framework. An excellent case in point: one of the most consistent demands of "anti-globalization" activists has been for the elimination of border restrictions. If we're to globalize, we say, let's get serious about it. Eliminate national borders. Let people come and go as they please, and live wherever they like. The demand is often phrased in terms of some notion of global citizenship. But this inspires immediate objections: doesn't a call for "global citizenship" mean calling for some kind of global state? Would we really want that? So then the question becomes how do we theorize a citizenship outside the state. This is often treated as a profound, perhaps insurmountable, dilemma; but if one considers the matter historically, it's hard to understand why it should be. Modern Western notions of citizenship and political freedoms are usually seen to derive from two traditions, one originating in ancient Athens, the other primarily stemming from medieval England (where it tends to be traced back to the assertion of aristocratic privilege against the Crown in the Magna Carta, Petition of Right, etc., and then the gradual extension of these same rights to the rest of the population). In fact there is no consensus among historians that either classical Athens or medieval England were states at all—and moreover, precisely for the reason that citizens' rights in the first, and aristocratic privilege in the second, were so well established. It is hard to think of Athens as a state, with a monopoly of force by the state apparatus, if one considers that the minimal government apparatus which did exist consisted entirely of slaves, owned collectively by the citizenry. Athens' police force consisted of Scythian archers imported from what's now Russia or Ukraine, and something of their legal standing might be gleaned from the fact that, by Athenian law, a slave's testimony was not admissible as evidence in court unless it was obtained under torture.

So what do we call such entities? "Chiefdoms"? One might conceivably be able to describe King John as a "chief" in the technical, evolutionary sense, but applying the term to Pericles does seem absurd. Neither can we continue to call ancient Athens a "city-state" if it wasn't a state at all. It seems we just don't have the intellectual tools to talk about such things. The same goes for the typology of types of state, or state-like entities in more recent times: an historian named Spruyt has suggested that in the sixteenth and seventeenth centuries the territorial nation-state was hardly the only game in town; there were other possibilities (Italian city-states, which actually were states; the Hanseatic league of confederated mercantile centers, which involved an entirely different conception of sovereignty) which didn't happen to win out—at least, right away—but were no less intrinsically viable. I have myself suggested that one reason the territorial nation-state ended up winning out was because, in this early stage of globalization, Western elites were trying to model themselves on China, the only state in existence at the time which actually seemed to conform to their ideal of a uniform population, who in Confucian terms were the source of sovereignty, creators of a vernacular literature, subject to a uniform code of laws, administered by bureaucrats chosen by merit, trained in that vernacular literature... With the current crisis of the nation-state and rapid increase in international institutions which are not exactly states, but in many ways just as obnoxious, juxta-posed against attempts to create international insti-tutions which do many of the same things as states but would be considerably less obnoxious, the lack of such a body of theory is becoming a genuine crisis.

3) YET ANOTHER THEORY OF CAPITALISM

One is loathe to suggest this but the endless drive to naturalize capitalism by reducing it to a matter of commercial calculation, which then allows one to claim it is as old as Sumer, just screams out for it. At the very least we need a proper theory of the history of wage labor, and relations like it. Since after all, it is in performing wage labor, not in buying and selling, that most humans now waste away most of their waking hours and it is that which makes them miserable. (Hence the IWW didn't say they were "anti-capitalist," much though they were; they got right to the point and said they were "against the wage system.") The earliest wage labor contracts we have on record appear to be really about the rental of slaves. What about a model of capitalism that sets out from that? Where anthropologists like Jonathan Friedman argue that ancient slavery was really just an older version of capitalism, we could just as easily—actually, a lot more easily—argue that modern capitalism is really just a newer version of slavery. Instead of people selling us or renting us out we rent out ourselves. But it's basically the same sort of arrangement.

4) POWER/IGNORANCE, or POWER/STUPIDITY

Academics love Michel Foucault's argument that identifies knowledge and power, and insists that brute force is no longer a major factor in social control. They love it because it flatters them: the perfect formula for people who like to think of themselves as political radicals even though all they do is write essays likely to be read by a few dozen other people in an institutional environment. Of course, if any of these academics were to walk into their university library to consult some volume of Foucault without having remembered to bring a valid ID, and decided to enter the stacks anyway, they would soon discover that brute force is really not so far away as they like to imagine—a man with a big stick, trained in exactly how hard to hit people with it, would rapidly appear to eject them.

In fact the threat of that man with the stick permeates our world at every moment; most of us have given up even thinking of crossing the innumerable lines and barriers he creates, just so we don't have to remind ourselves of his existence. If you see a hungry woman standing several yards away from a huge pile of food—a daily occurrence for most of us who live in cities—there is a reason you can't just take some and give it to her. A man with a big stick will come and very likely hit you. Anarchists, in contrast, have always delighted in reminding us of him. Residents of the squatter community of Christiana, Denmark, for example, have a Christmastide ritual where they dress in Santa suits, take toys from department stores and distribute them to children on the street, partly just so everyone can relish the images of the cops beating down Santa and snatching the toys back from crying children.

Such a theoretical emphasis opens the way to a theory of the relation of power not with knowledge, but with ignorance and stupidity. Because violence, particularly structural violence, where all the power is on one side, creates ignorance. If you have the power to hit people over the head whenever you want, you don't have to trouble yourself too much figuring out what they think is going on, and therefore, generally speaking, you don't. Hence the sure-fire way to simplify social arrangements, to ignore the incredibly complex play of perspectives, passions, insights, desires, and mutual understandings that human life is really made of, is to make a rule and threaten to attack anyone who breaks it. This is why violence has always been the favored recourse of the stupid: it is the one form of stupidity to which it is almost impossible to come up with an intelligent response. It is also of course the basis of the state.

Contrary to popular belief, bureaucracies do not create stupidity. They are ways of managing situations that are already inherently stupid because they are, ultimately, based on the arbitrariness of force.

Ultimately this should lead to a theory of the relation of violence and the imagination. Why is it that the folks on the bottom (the victims of structural violence) are always imagining what it must be like for the folks on top (the beneficiaries of structural violence), but it almost never occurs to the folks on top to wonder what it might be like to be on the bottom? Human beings being the sympathetic creatures that they are this tends to become one of the main bastions of any system of inequality—the downtrodden actually care about their oppressors, at least, far more than their oppressors care about them—but this seems itself to be an effect of structural violence.

5) AN ECOLOGY OF VOLUNTARY ASSOCIATIONS

What kinds exist? In what environments do they thrive? Where did the bizarre notion of the "corporation" come from anyway?

6) A THEORY OF POLITICAL HAPPINESS

Rather than just a theory of why most contemporary people never experience it. That would be easy.

7) HIERARCHY

A theory of how structures of hierarchy, by their own logic, necessarily create their own counter-image or negation. They do, you know.

8) SUFFERING AND PLEASURE: ON THE PRIVATIZATION OF DESIRE

It is common wisdom among anarchists, autono-mists, Situationists, and other new revolutionaries that the old breed of grim, determined, self-sacri-ficing revolutionary, who sees the world only in terms of suffering will ultimately only produce more suffering himself. Certainly that's what has tended to happen in the past. Hence the emphasis on pleasure, carnival, on creating "temporary autonomous zones" where one can live as if one is already free. The ideal of the "festival of resistance" with its crazy music and giant puppets is, quite consciously, to return to the late medieval world of huge wickerwork giants and dragons, maypoles and morris dancing; the very world the Puritan pioneers of the "capitalist spirit" hated so much and ulti-mately managed to destroy. The history of capi-talism moves from attacks on collective, festive consumption to the promulgation of highly personal, private, even furtive forms (after all, once they had all those people dedicating all their time to producing stuff instead of partying, they did have to figure out a way to sell it all); a process of the privitization of desire. The theoretical question: how to reconcile all this with the disturbing theo-retical insight of people like Slavoj Žižek: that if one wishes to inspire ethnic hatred, the easiest way to do so is to concentrate on the bizarre, perverse ways in which the other group is assumed to pursue pleasure. If one wishes to emphasize commonality, the easiest way is to point out that they also feel pain.

9) ONE OR SEVERAL THEORIES OF ALIENATION

This is the ultimate prize: what, precisely, are the possible dimensions of non-alienated experience? How might its modalities be catalogued, or considered? Any anarchist anthropology worth its salt would have to pay particular attention to this question because this is precisely what all those punks, hippies, and activists of every stripe most look to anthropology to learn. It's the anthropologists, so terrified of being accused of romanticizing the societies they study that they refuse to even suggest there might be an answer, who leave them no recourse but to fall into the arms of the real romanticizers. Primitivists like John Zerzan, who in trying to whittle away what seems to divide us from pure, unmediated experience, end up whittling away absolutely everything. Zerzan's increasingly popular works end up condemning the very existence of language, math, time keeping, music, and all forms of art and representation. They are all written off as forms of alienation, leaving us with a kind of impossible evolutionary ideal: the only truly non-alienated human being was not even quite human, but more a kind of perfect ape, in some kind of currently-unimaginable telepathic connection with its fellows, at one with wild nature, living maybe about a hundred thousand years ago. True revolution could only mean somehow returning to that. How it is that afficionados of this sort of thing still manage to engage in effective political action (because it's been my experience that many do quite remarkable work) is itself a fascinating sociological question. But surely, an alternative analysis of alienation might be useful here.

We could start with a kind of sociology of micro-utopias, the counterpart of a parallel typology of forms of alienation, alienated and non-alienated forms of action... The moment we stop insisting on viewing all forms of action only by their function in reproducing larger, total, forms of inequality of power, we will also be able to see that anarchist social relations and non-alien-ated forms of action are all around us. And this is critical because it already shows that anarchism is, already, and has always been, one of the main bases for human interaction. We self-organize and engage in mutual aid all the time. We always have. We also engage in artistic creativity, which I think if examined would reveal that many of the least alienated forms of experience do usually involve an element of what a Marxist would call fetishization. It is all the more pressing to develop such a theory if you accept that (as I have frequently argued) revolutionary constituencies always involve a tacit alliance between the least alienated and the most oppressed.

Q: How many voters does it take to change a light bulb?

A: None. Because voters can't change anything.

There is of course no single anarchist program—nor could there really be—but it might be helpful to end by giving the reader some idea about current directions of thought and organizing.

(1) Globalization and the Elimination of North-South Inequalities

As I've mentioned, the "anti-globalization movement" is increasingly anarchist in inspiration. In the long run the anarchist position on globalization is obvious: the effacement of nation-states will mean the elimination of national borders. This is genuine globalization. Anything else is just a sham. But for the interim, there are all sorts of concrete suggestions on how the situation can be improved right now, without falling back on statist, protectionist, approaches. One example:

Once during the protests before the World Economic Forum, a kind of junket of tycoons, corporate flacks and politicians, networking and sharing cocktails at the Waldorf Astoria, pretended to be discussing ways to alleviate global poverty. I was invited to engage in a radio debate with one of their representatives. As it happened the task went to another activist but I did get far enough to prepare a three-point program that I think would have taken care of the problem nicely:

- an immediate amnesty on international debt (An amnesty on personal debt might not be a bad idea either but it's a different issue.)
- an immediate cancellation of all patents and other intellectual property rights related to technology more than one year old
- the elimination of all restrictions on global freedom of travel or residence

The rest would pretty much take care of itself. The moment the average resident of Tanzania, or Laos, was no longer forbidden to relocate to Minneapolis or Rotterdam, the government of every rich and powerful country in the world would certainly decide nothing was more important than finding a way to make sure people in Tanzania and Laos preferred to stay there. Do you really think they couldn't come up with something?

The point is that despite the endless rhetoric about "complex, subtle, intractable issues" (justifying decades of expensive research by the rich and their well-paid flunkies), the anarchist program would probably have resolved most of them in five or six years. But, you will say, these demands are entirely unrealistic! True enough. But why are they unrealistic? Mainly, because those rich guys meeting in the Waldorf would never stand for any of it. This is why we say they are themselves the problem.

(2) The Struggle Against Work

The struggle against work has always been central to anarchist organizing. By this I mean, not the struggle for better worker conditions or higher wages, but the struggle to eliminate work, as a relation of domination, entirely. Hence the IWW slogan "against the wage system." This is a long-term goal of course. In the shorter term, what can't be eliminated can at least be reduced. Around the turn of the century, the Wobblies and other anarchists played the central role in winning workers the 5-day week and 8-hour day.

In Western Europe social democratic governments are now, for the first time in almost a century, once again reducing the working week. They are only instituting trifling changes (from a 40-hour week to 35), but in the US no one's even discussing that much. Instead they are discussing whether to eliminate time-and-a-half for overtime. This despite the fact that Americans now spend more hours working than any other population in the world, including Japan. So the Wobblies have reappeared, with what was to be the next step in their program, even back in the '20s: the 16-hour week. ("4-day week, 4-hour day.") Again, on the face of it, this seems completely unrealistic, even insane. But has anyone carried out a feasibility study? After all, it has been repeatedly demonstrated that a considerable chunk of the hours worked in America are only actually necessary to compensate for problems created by the fact that Americans work too much. (Consider here such jobs as all-night pizza deliveryman or dog-washer, or those women who run nighttime day care centers for the children of women who have to work nights providing child care for businesswomen...not to mention the endless hours spent by specialists cleaning up the emotional and physical damage caused by overwork, the injuries, suicides, divorces, murderous rampages, producing the drugs to pacify the children...)

So what jobs are really necessary?

Well, for starters, there are lots of jobs whose disappearance, almost everyone would agree, would be a net gain for humanity. Consider here telemarketers, stretch-SUV manufacturers, or for that matter, corporate lawyers. We could also eliminate the entire advertising and PR industries, fire all politicians and their staffs, eliminate anyone remotely connected with an HMO, without even beginning to get near essential social functions. The elimination of advertising would also reduce the production, shipping, and selling of unnecessary products, since those items people actually do want or need, they will still figure out a way to find out about. The elimination of radical inequalities would mean we would no longer require the services of most of the millions currently employed as doormen, private security forces, prison guards, or SWAT teams—not to mention the military. Beyond that, we'd have to do research. Financiers, insurers, and investment bankers are all essentially parasitic beings, but there might be some useful functions in these sectors that could not simply be replaced with software. All in all we might discover that if we identified the work that really did need to be done to maintain a comfortable and ecologically sustainable standard of living, and redistribute the hours, it may turn out that the Wobbly platform is perfectly realistic. Especially if we bear in mind that it's not like anyone would be forced to stop working after four hours if they didn't feel like it. A lot of people do enjoy their jobs, certainly more than they would lounging around doing nothing all day (that's why in prisons, when they want to punish inmates, they take away their right to work), and if one has eliminated the endless indignities and sadomasochistic games that inevitably follow from top-down organization, one would expect a lot more would. It might even turn out that no one will have to work more than they particularly want to.

minor note:
Admittedly, all of this presumes the total reorganization of work, a kind of "after the revolution" scenario which I've argued is a necessary tool to even begin to think about human possibilities, even

if revolution will probably never take such an apocalyptic form. This of course brings up the "who
will do the dirty jobs?" question—one which
always gets thrown at anarchists or other utopians.
Peter Kropotkin long ago pointed out the fallacy
of the argument. There's no particular reason dirty
jobs have to exist. If one divided up the unpleasant
tasks equally, that would mean all the world's top
scientists and engineers would have to do them
too; one could expect the creation of self-cleaning
kitchens and coal-mining robots almost immediately.

All this is something of an aside though because what
I really want to do in this final section is focus on:

(3) DEMOCRACY

This might give the reader a chance to have a glance
at what anarchist, and anarchist-inspired, organizing is
actually like—some of the contours of the new world
now being built in the shell of the old—and to show
what the historical-ethnographic perspective I've been
trying to develop here, our non-existent science,
might be able to contribute to it.

The first cycle of the new global uprising—
what the press still insists on referring to, increasingly
ridiculously, as "the anti-globalization movement"—
began with the autonomous municipalities of Chiapas
and came to a head with the *asambleas barreales* of
Buenos Aires, and cities throughout Argentina. There
is hardly room here to tell the whole story: beginning

with the Zapatistas' rejection of the idea of seizing power and their attempt instead to create a model of democratic self-organization to inspire the rest of Mexico; their initiation of an international network (People's Global Action, or PGA) which then put out the calls for days of action against the WTO (in Seattle), IMF (in Washington, Prague...) and so on; and finally, the collapse of the Argentine economy, and the overwhelming popular uprising which, again, rejected the very idea that one could find a solution by replacing one set of politicians with another. The slogan of the Argentine movement was, from the start, *que se vayan todas*—get rid of the lot of them. Instead of a new government they created a vast network of alternative institutions, starting with popular assemblies to govern each urban neighborhood (the only limitation on participation is that one cannot be employed by a political party), hundreds of occupied, worker-managed factories, a complex system of "barter" and newfangled alternative currency system to keep them in operation—in short, an endless variation on the theme of direct democracy.

All of this has happened completely below the radar screen of the corporate media, which also missed the point of the great mobilizations. The organization of these actions was meant to be a living illustration of what a truly democratic world might be like, from the festive puppets to the careful organization of affinity groups and spokescouncils, all operating without a leadership structure, always based on principles of consensus-based direct democracy. It was the kind of organization which most people would have, had they simply heard it proposed, written off as a pipe-dream; but it worked, and so effectively that the police departments of city after city were completely flummoxed with how to deal with them. Of course, this also had something to do with the unprecedented tactics (hundreds of activists in fairy suits tickling police with feather dusters, or padded with so many inflatable inner tubes and rubber cushions they seemed to roll along like the Michelin man over barricades, incapable of damaging anyone else but also pretty much impervious to police batons...), which completely confused traditional categories of violence and nonviolence.

When protesters in Seattle chanted "this is what democracy looks like," they meant to be taken literally. In the best tradition of direct action, they not only confronted a certain form of power, exposing its mechanisms and attempting literally to stop it in its tracks: they did it in a way which demonstrated why the kind of social relations on which it is based were unnecessary. This is why all the condescending remarks about the movement being dominated by a bunch of dumb kids with no coherent ideology completely missed the mark. The diversity was a function of the decentralized form of organization, and this organization *was* the movement's ideology.

The key term in the new movement is "process," by which is meant, decision-making process. In North America, this is almost invariably done through some process of finding consensus. This is as I mentioned much less ideologically stifling than it may sound because the assumption behind all good consensus process is that one should not even try to convert others to one's overall point of view; the point of consensus process is to allow a group to decide on a common course of action. Instead of voting proposals up and down, then, proposals are worked and reworked, scotched or reinvented, until one ends up with something everyone can live with. When it comes to the final stage, actually "finding consensus," there are two levels of possible objection: one can "stand aside," which is to say "I don't like this and won't participate but I wouldn't stop anyone else from doing it," or "block," which has the effect of a veto. One can only block if one feels a proposal is in violation of the fundamental principles or reasons for being of a group. One might say that the function which in the US constitution is relegated to the courts, of striking down legislative decisions that violate constitutional principles, is here relegated to anyone with the courage to actually stand up against the combined will of the group (though of course there are also ways of challenging unprincipled blocks).

One could go on at length about the elaborate and surprisingly sophisticated methods that have been developed to ensure all this works; of forms of modified consensus required for very large groups; of the way consensus itself reinforces the principle of decentralization by ensuring one doesn't really want to bring proposals before very large groups unless one has to, of means of ensuring gender equity and resolving conflict... The point is this is a form of direct democracy which is very different than the kind we usually associate with the term—or, for that matter, with the kind usually employed by European or North

American anarchists of earlier generations, or still employed, say, in urban Argentine *asambleas*. In North America, consensus process emerged more than anything else through the feminist movement, as part of broad backlash against some of the more obnoxious, self-aggrandizing macho leadership styles of the '60s New Left. Much of the procedure was originally adopted from the Quakers, and Quaker-inspired groups; the Quakers, in turn, claim to have been inspired by Native American practice. How much the latter is really true is, in historical terms, difficult to determine. Nonetheless, Native American decision-making did normally work by some form of consensus. Actually, so do most popular assemblies around the world now, from the Tzeltal or Tzotzil or Tojolobal-speaking communities in Chiapas to Malagasy *fokon'olona*. After having lived in Madagascar for two years, I was startled, the first time I started attending meetings of the Direct Action Network in New York, by how familiar it all seemed—the main difference was that the DAN process was so much more formalized and explicit. It had to be, since everyone in DAN was just figuring out how to make decisions this way, and everything had to be spelled out; whereas in Madagascar, everyone had been doing this since they learned to speak.

In fact, as anthropologists are aware, just about every known human community which has to come to group decisions has employed some variation of what I'm calling "consensus process"—every one, that is, which is not in some way or another drawing on the tradition of ancient Greece. Majoritarian democracy, in the formal, Roberts Rules of Order-type sense rarely emerges of its own accord. It's curious that almost no one, anthropologists included, ever seems to ask oneself why this should be.

An hypothesis.
Majoritarian democracy was, in its origins, essentially a military institution.

Of course it's the peculiar bias of Western historiography that this is the only sort of democracy that is seen to count as "democracy" at all. We are usually told that democracy originated in ancient Athens—like science, or philosophy, it was a Greek invention. It's never entirely clear what this is supposed to mean. Are we supposed to believe that before the Athenians, it never really occurred to anyone, anywhere, to gather all the members of their community in order to make joint decisions in a way that gave everyone equal say? That would be ridiculous. Clearly there have been plenty of egalitarian societies in history—many far more egalitarian than Athens, many that must have existed before 500 BCE—and obviously, they must have had some kind of procedure for coming to decisions for matters of collective importance. Yet somehow, it is always assumed that these procedures, whatever they might have been, could not have been, properly speaking, "democratic."

Even scholars with otherwise impeccable radical credentials, promoters of direct democracy, have been known to bend themselves into pretzels trying to justify this attitude. Non-Western egali-

tarian communities are "kin-based," argues
Murray Bookchin. (And Greece was not? Of
course the Athenian agora was not itself kin-based
but neither is a Malagasy *fokon'olona* or Balinese
seka. So what?) "Some might speak of Iroquois or
Berber democracy," argued Cornelius Castoriadis,
"but this is an abuse of the term. These are primitive societies which assume the social order is
handed to them by gods or spirits, not self-consti-
tuted by the people themselves as in Athens."
(Really? In fact the "League of the Iroquois" was a
treaty organization, seen as a common agreement
created in historical times, and subject to constant
renegotiation.) The arguments never make sense.
But they don't really have to because we are not
really dealing with arguments at all here, so much
as with the brush of a hand.

The real reason for the unwillingness of most
scholars to see a Sulawezi or Tallensi village council
as "democratic"—well, aside from simple racism,
the reluctance to admit anyone Westerners slaughtered with such relative impunity were quite on the
level as Pericles—is that they do not vote. Now,
admittedly, this is an interesting fact. Why not? If
we accept the idea that a show of hands, or having
everyone who supports a proposition stand on one
side of the plaza and everyone against stand on the
other, are not really such incredibly sophisticated
ideas that they never would have occurred to
anyone until some ancient genius "invented" them,
then why are they so rarely employed? Again, we
seem to have an example of explicit rejection. Over
and over, across the world, from Australia to
Siberia, egalitarian communities have preferred
some variation on consensus process. Why?

The explanation I would propose is this: it is much easier, in a face-to-face community, to figure out what most members of that community want to do, than to figure out how to convince those who do not to go along with it. Consensus decision-making is typical of societies where there would be no way to compel a minority to agree with a majority decision—either because there is no state with a monopoly of coercive force, or because the state has nothing to do with local decision-making. If there is no way to compel those who find a majority decision distasteful to go along with it, then the last thing one would want to do is to hold a vote: a public contest which someone will be seen to lose. Voting would be the most likely means to guarantee humiliations, resentments, hatreds, in the end, the destruction of communities. What is seen as an elaborate and difficult process of finding consensus is, in fact, a long process of making sure no one walks away feeling that their views have been totally ignored.

Majority democracy, we might say, can only emerge when two factors coincide:

1. a feeling that people should have equal say in making group decisions, and
2. a coercive apparatus capable of enforcing those decisions.

For most of human history, it has been extremely unusual to have both at the same time. Where egalitarian societies exist, it is also usually considered wrong to impose systematic coercion. Where a machinery of coercion did exist, it did not even occur to those wielding it that they were enforcing any sort of popular will.

It is of obvious relevance that Ancient Greece was one of the most competitive societies known to history. It was a society that tended to make everything into a public contest, from athletics to philosophy or tragic drama or just about anything else. So it might not seem entirely surprising that they made political decision-making into a public contest as well. Even more crucial though was the fact that decisions were made by a populace in arms. Aristotle, in his *Politics*, remarks that the constitution of a Greek city-state will normally depend on the chief arm of its military: if this is cavalry, it will be an aristocracy, since horses are expensive. If hoplite infantry, it will have an oligarchy, as all could not afford the armor and training. If its power was based in the navy or light infantry, one could expect a democracy, as anyone can row, or use a sling. In other words if a man is armed, then one pretty much has to take his opinions into account. One can see how this worked at its starkest in Xenophon's *Anabasis*, which tells the story of an army of Greek mercenaries who suddenly find themselves leaderless and lost in the middle of Persia. They elect new officers, and then hold a collective vote to decide what to do next. In a case like this, even if the vote was 60/40, everyone could see the balance of forces and what would happen if things actually came to blows. Every vote was, in a real sense, a conquest.

Roman legions could be similarly democratic; this was the main reason they were never allowed to enter the city of Rome. And when Machiavelli revived the notion of a democratic republic at the dawn of the "modern" era, he immediately reverted to the notion of a populace in arms.

This in turn might help explain the term "democracy" itself, which appears to have been coined as something of a slur by its elitist opponents: it literally means the "force" or even "violence" of the people. *Kratos*, not *archos*. The elitists who coined the term always considered democracy not too far from simple rioting or mob rule; though of course their solution was the permanent conquest of the people by someone else. And ironically, when they did manage to suppress democracy for this reason, which was usually, the result was that the only way the general populace's will was known was precisely through rioting, a practice that became quite institutionalized in, say, imperial Rome or eighteenth-century England.

All this is not to say that direct democracies—as practiced, for example, in medieval cities or New England town meetings—were not normally orderly and dignified procedures; though one suspects that here too, in actual practice, there was a certain baseline of consensus-seeking going on. Still, it was this military undertone which allowed the authors of the *Federalist Papers*, like almost all other literate men of their day, to take it for granted that what they called "democracy"—by which they meant, direct democracy—was in its nature the most unstable, tumultuous form of government, not to mention one which endangers the rights of minorities (the specific minority they had in mind in this case being the rich). It was only once the term "democracy" could be almost completely transformed to incorporate the principle of representation—a term which itself has a very curious history, since as Cornelius Castoriadis notes, it originally referred to representatives of the people before the king, internal ambassadors in fact, rather than those who wielded power in any sense themselves—that it was rehabilitated, in the eyes of well-born political theorists, and took on the meaning it has today.

In a sense then anarchists think all those right-wing political theorists who insist that "America is not a democracy; it's a republic" are quite correct. The difference is that anarchists have a problem with that. They think it ought to be a democracy. Though increasing numbers have come to accept that the traditional elitist criticism of majoritarian direct democracy is not entirely baseless either.

I noted earlier that all social orders are in some sense at war with themselves. Those unwilling to establish an apparatus of violence for enforcing decisions necessarily have to develop an apparatus for creating and maintaining social consensus (at least in that minimal sense of ensuring malcontents can still feel they have freely chosen to go along with bad decisions); as an apparent result, the internal war ends up projected outwards into endless night battles and forms of spectral violence. Majoritarian direct democracy is constantly threatening to make those lines of force explicit. For this reason it does tend to be rather unstable: or more precisely, if it does last, it's because its institutional forms (the medieval city, New England town council, for that matter gallup polls, referendums...) are almost invariably ensconced within a larger framework of governance in which ruling elites use that very instability to justify their ultimate monopoly of the means of violence. Finally, the threat of this instability becomes an excuse for a form of "democracy" so minimal that it comes down to nothing more than insisting that ruling elites should occasionally consult with "the public"—in carefully staged contests, replete with rather meaningless jousts and tournaments—to reestablish their right to go on making their decisions for them.

It's a trap. Bouncing back and forth between the two ensures it will remain extremely unlikely that one could ever imagine it would be possible for people to manage their own lives, without the help of "representatives." It's for this reason the new global movement has begun by reinventing the very meaning of democracy. To do so ultimately means, once again, coming to terms with the fact that "we"—whether as "the West" (whatever that means), as the "modern world," or anything else—are not really as special as we like to think we are; that we're not the only people ever to have practiced democracy; that in fact, rather than disseminating democracy around the world, "Western" governments have been spending at least as much time inserting themselves into the lives of people who have been practicing democracy for thousands of years, and in one way or another, telling them to cut it out.

One of the most encouraging things about these new, anarchist-inspired movements is that they propose a new form of internationalism. Older, communist internationalism had some very beautiful ideals, but in organizational terms, everyone basically flowed one way. It became a means for regimes outside Europe and its settler colonies to learn Western styles of organization: party structures, plenaries, purges, bureaucratic hierarchies, secret police... This time—the second wave of internationalism one could call it, or just, anarchist globalization—the movement of organizational forms has largely gone the other way. It's not just consensus process: the idea of mass non-violent direct action first developed in South Africa and India; the current network model was first proposed by rebels in Chiapas; even the notion of the affinity group came out of Spain and Latin America. The fruits of ethnography—and the techniques of ethnography—could be enormously helpful here if anthropologists can get past their—however understandable—hesitancy, owing to their own often squalid colonial history, and come to see what they are sitting on not as some guilty secret (which is nonetheless their guilty secret, and no one else's) but as the common property of humankind.

ANTHROPOLOGY
(in which the author somewhat reluctantly bites the hand that feeds him)

The final question—one that I've admittedly been rather avoiding up to now—is why anthropologists haven't, so far? I have already described why I think academics, in general, have rarely felt much affinity with anarchism. I've talked a little about the radical inclinations in much early twentieth-century anthropology, which often showed a very strong affinity with anarchism, but that seemed to largely evaporate over time. It's all a little odd. Anthropologists are after all the only group of scholars who know anything about actually-existing stateless societies; many have actually lived in corners of the world where states have ceased to function or at least temporarily pulled up stakes and left, and people are managing their own affairs autonomously; if nothing else, they are keenly aware that the most commonplace assumptions about what would happen in the absence of a state ("but people would just kill each other!") are factually untrue.

Why, then?

Well, there are any number of reasons. Some are understandable enough. If anarchism is, essentially, an ethics of practice, then meditating on anthropological practice tends to kick up a lot of unpleasant things. Particularly if one concentrates on the experience of anthropological fieldwork—which is what anthropologists invariably tend to do when they become reflexive. The discipline we know today was made possible by horrific schemes of conquest, colonization, and mass murder—much like most modern academic disciplines, actually, including geography, and botany, not even to mention ones like mathematics, linguistics or robotics, which still are, but anthropologists, since their work tends to involve getting to know the victims personally, have ended up agonizing over this in ways that the proponents of other disciplines have almost never done. The result has been strangely paradoxical: anthropological reflections on their own culpability has mainly had the effect of providing non-anthropologists who do not want to be bothered having to learn about 90% of human experience with a handy two or three sentence dismissal (you know: all about projecting one's sense of Otherness into the colonized) by which they can feel morally superior to those who do.

For the anthropologists themselves, the results have been strangely paradoxical as well. While anthropologists are, effectively, sitting on a vast archive of human experience, of social and political experiments no one else really knows about, that very body of comparative ethnography is seen as something shameful. As I mentioned, it is treated not as the common heritage of humankind, but as our dirty little secret. Which is actually convenient, at least insofar as academic power is largely about establishing ownership rights over a certain form of knowledge and ensuring that others don't really have much access to it. Because as I also mentioned, our dirty little secret is still ours. It's not something one needs to share with others.

There's more to it though. In many ways, anthropology seems a discipline terrified of its own potential. It is, for example, the only discipline in a position to make generalizations about humanity as a whole—since it is the only discipline that actually takes all of humanity into account, and is familiar with all the anomalous cases. ("All societies practice marriage, you say? Well that depends on how you define 'marriage.' Among the Nayar...") Yet it resolutely refuses to do so. I don't think this is to be accounted for solely as an understandable reaction to the right-wing proclivity to make grand arguments about human nature to justify very particular, and usually, particularly nasty social institutions (rape, war, free market capitalism)—though certainly that is a big part of it. Partly it's just the vastness of the subject matter. Who really has the means, in discussing, say, conceptions of desire, or imagination, or the self, or sovereignty, to consider everything Chinese or Indian or Islamic thinkers have had to say on the matter in addition to the Western canon, let alone folk conceptions prevalent in hundreds of Oceanic or Native American societies as well? It's just too daunting. As a result, anthropologists no longer produce many broad theoretical generalizations at all—instead, turning over the work to European philosophers who usually have absolutely no problem discussing desire, or the imagination, or the self, or sovereignty, as if such concepts had been invented by Plato or Aristotle, developed by Kant or DeSade, and never meaningfully discussed by anyone outside of elite literary traditions in Western Europe or North America. Where once anthropologists' key theoretical terms were words like mana, totem, or taboo, the new buzzwords are invariably derived from Latin or Greek, usually via French, occasionally German.

So while anthropology might seem perfectly positioned to provide an intellectual forum for all sorts of planetary conversations, political and otherwise, there is a certain built-in reluctance to do so.

Then there's the question of politics. Most anthropologists write as if their work has obvious political significance, in a tone which suggests they consider what they are doing quite radical, and certainly left of center. But what does this politics actually consist of? It's increasingly hard to say. Do anthropologists tend to be anti-capitalist? Certainly it's hard to think of one who has much good to say about capitalism. Many are in the habit of describing the current age as one of "late capitalism," as if by declaring it is about to end, they can by the very act of doing so hasten its demise. But it's hard to think of an anthropologist who has, recently, made any sort of suggestion of what an alternative to capitalism might be like. So are they liberals? Many can't pronounce the word without a snort of contempt. What then? As far as I can make out the only real fundamental political commitment running through the entire field is a kind of broad populism. If nothing else, we are definitely not on the side of whoever, in a given situation, is or fancies themselves to be the elite. We're for the little guys. Since in practice, most anthropologists are attached to (increasingly global) universities, or if not, end up in jobs like marketing consultancies or jobs with the UN—positions within the very apparatus of global rule—what this really comes down to is a kind of constant, ritualized declaration of disloyalty to that very global elite of which we ourselves, as academics, clearly form one (admittedly somewhat marginal) fraction.

Now, what form does this populism take in practice? Mainly, it means that you must demonstrate that the people you are studying, the little guys, are successfully resisting some form of power or globalizing influence imposed on them from above. This is, anyway, what most anthropologists talk about when the subject turns to globalization—which it usually does almost immediately, nowadays, whatever it is you study. Whether it is advertising, or soap operas, or forms of labor discipline, or state-imposed legal systems, or anything else that might seem to be crushing or homogenizing or manipulating one's people, one demonstrates that they are not fooled, not crushed, not homogenized; indeed they are creatively appropriating or reinterpreting what is being thrown at them in ways that its authors would never have anticipated. Of course, to some extent all this is true. I would certainly not wish to deny it is important to combat the—still remarkably widespread—popular assumption that the moment people in Bhutan or Irian Jaya are exposed to MTV, their civilization is basically over. What's disturbing, at least to me, is the degree to which this logic comes to echo that of global capitalism. Advertising agencies, after all, do not claim to be imposing anything on the public either. Particularly in this era of market segmentation, they claim to be providing material for members of the public to appropriate and make their own in unpredictable and idiosyncratic ways. The rhetoric of "creative consumption" in particular could be considered the very ideology of the new global market: a world in which all human behavior can be classified as either production, exchange, or consumption; in which exchange is assumed to be driven by basic human proclivities for rational pursuit of profit which are the same everywhere, and consumption becomes a way to establish one's particular identity (and production is not discussed at all if one can possibly avoid it). We're all the same on the trading floor; it's what we do with the stuff when we get home that makes us different. This market logic has become so deeply internalized that, if, say, a woman in Trinidad puts together some outrageous get-up and goes out dancing, anthropologists will automatically assume that what she's doing can be defined as "consumption" (as opposed to, say, showing off or having a good time), as if what's really important about her evening is the fact that she buys a couple drinks, or maybe, because the anthropologist considers wearing clothes itself to be somehow like drinking, or maybe, because they just don't think about it at all and assume that whatever one does that isn't working is "consumption" because what's really important about it is that manufactured products are involved. The perspective of the anthropologist and the global marketing executive have become almost indistinguishable.

It's not that different on the political level. Lauren Leve has recently warned that anthropologists risk, if they are not careful, becoming yet another cog in a global "identity machine," a planet-wide apparatus of institutions and assumptions that has, over the last decade or so, effectively informed the earth's inhabitants (or at least, all but the very most elite) that, since all debates about the nature of political or economic possibilities are now over, the only way one can now make a political claim is by asserting some group identity, with all the assumptions about what identity is (i.e., that group identities are not ways of comparing one group to each other but constituted by the way a group relates to its own history, that there is no essential difference in this regard between individuals and groups...) established in advance. Things have come to such a pass that in countries like Nepal even Theravada Buddhists are forced to play identity politics, a particularly bizarre spectacle since they are essentially basing their identity claims on adherence to a universalistic philosophy that insists identity is an illusion.

Many years ago a French anthropologist named Gerard Althabe wrote a book about Madagascar called *Oppression et Liberation dans l'Imaginaire*. It's a catchy phrase. I think it might well be applied to what ends up happening in a lot of anthropological writing. For the most part, what we call "identities" here, in what Paul Gilroy likes to call the "over-developed world," are forced on people. In the United States, most are the products of ongoing oppression and inequality: someone who is defined as Black is not allowed to forget that during a single moment of their existence; his or her own self-definition is of no significance to the banker who will deny him credit, or the policeman who will arrest him for being in the wrong neighborhood, or the doctor who, in the case of a damaged limb, will be more likely to recommend amputation. All attempts at individual or collective self-fashioning or self-invention have to take place entirely within those extremely violent sets of constraints. (The only real way that could change would be to transform the attitudes of those who have the privilege of being defined as "White"—ultimately, probably, by destroying the category of Whiteness itself.) The fact is though that nobody has any idea how most people in North America would chose to define themselves if institutional racism were to actually vanish—if everyone really were left free to define themselves however they wished. Neither is there much point in speculating about it. The question is how to create a situation where we could find out.

This is what I mean by "liberation in the imaginary." To think about what it would take to live in a world in which everyone really did have the power to decide for themselves, individually and collectively, what sort of communities they wished to belong to and what sort of identities they wanted to take on—that's really difficult. To bring about such a world would be almost unimaginably difficult. It would require changing almost everything. It also would meet with stubborn, and ultimately violent, opposition from those who benefit the most from existing arrangements. To instead write as if these identities are already freely created—or largely so—is easy, and it lets one entirely off the hook for the intricate and intractable problems of the degree to which one's own work is part of this very identity machine. But it no more makes it true than talking about "late capitalism" will itself bring about industrial collapse or further social revolution.

An illustration:

In case it's not clear what I am saying here, let me return for a moment to the Zapatista rebels of Chiapas, whose revolt on New Year's day, 1994, might be said to have kicked off what came to be known as the globalization movement. The Zapatistas were overwhelmingly drawn from Tzeltal, Tzotzil and Tojolobal Maya-speaking communities that had established themselves in the Lacandon rain forest—some of the poorest and most exploited communities in Mexico. The Zapatistas do not call themselves anarchists, quite, or even, quite autonomists; they represent their own unique strand within that broader tradition; indeed, they are trying to revolutionize revolutionary strategy itself by abandoning any notion of a vanguard party seizing control of the state, but instead battling to create free enclaves that could serve as models for autonomous self-government, allowing a general reorganization of Mexican society into a complex overlapping network of self-managing groups that could then begin to discuss the reinvention of political society. There was, apparently, some difference of opinion within the Zapatista movement itself over the forms of democratic practice they wished to promulgate. The Maya-speaking base pushed strongly for a form of consensus process adopted from their own communal traditions, but reformulated to be more radically egalitarian; some of the Spanish-speaking military leadership of the rebellion were highly skeptical of whether this could really be applied on the national level. Ultimately, though, they had to defer to the vision of those they "led by obeying," as the Zapatista saying went. But the remarkable thing was what happened when news of this rebellion spread to the rest of the world. It's here we can really see the workings of Leve's "identity machine." Rather than a band of rebels with a vision of radical democratic transformation, they were immediately redefined as a band of Mayan Indians demanding indigenous autonomy. This is how the international media portrayed them; this is what was considered important about them from everyone from humanitarian organizations to Mexican bureaucrats to human rights monitors at the UN. As time went on, the Zapatistas—whose strategy has from the beginning been dependent on gaining allies in the international community— were increasingly forced to play the indigenous card as well, except when dealing with their most committed allies.

This strategy has not been entirely ineffective. Ten years later, the Zapatista Army of National Liberation is still there, without having hardly had to fire a shot, if only because they have been willing, for the time being, to downplay the "National" part in their name. All I want to emphasize is exactly how patronizing—or, maybe let's not pull punches here, how completely racist—the international reaction to the Zapatista rebellion has really been. Because what the Zapatistas were proposing to do was exactly to begin that difficult work that, I pointed out, so much of the rhetoric about "identity" effectively ignores: trying to work out what forms of organization, what forms of process and deliberation, would be required to create a world in which people and communities are actually free to determine for themselves what sort of people and communities they wish to be. And what were they told? Effectively, they were informed that, since they were Maya, they could not possibly have anything to say to the world about the processes through which identity is constructed; or about the nature of political possibilities. As Mayas, the only possible political statement they could make to non-Mayas would be about their Maya identity itself. They could assert the right to continue to be Mayan. They could demand recognition as Mayan. But for a Maya to say something to the world that was not simply a comment on their own Maya-ness would be inconceivable.

And who was listening to what they really had to say?

Largely, it seems, a collection of teenage anarchists in Europe and North America, who soon began besieging the summits of the very global elite to whom anthropologists maintain such an uneasy, uncomfortable, alliance.

But the anarchists were right. I think anthropologists should make common cause with them. We have tools at our fingertips that could be of enormous importance for human freedom. Let's start taking some responsibility for it. ■

Also available from Prickly Paradigm Press:

continued

continued